THE
ILIAD
and the
ODYSSEY

ISBN 0-86163-597-3

Published by Award Publications Limited,
Spring House, Spring Place, Kertish Town,
London NWS 3BH, England

Copyright © 1992 Dami Editore, Milano

Printed in Italy

Stampa Officine Grafiche De Agostini - 1992
Confezione Legatoria del Verbano

THE
ILIAD
and the
ODYSSEY

Award Publications Limited

Part one
THE ILIAD

page 7

Part two
THE ODYSSEY

page 81

THE
ILIAD

A terrible row breaks out between Achilles and Agamemnon

BOOK I

For nine years war had been raging under the walls of Troy. For nine years Greeks and Trojans had been engaged in a terrible war without one or the other being favoured by a decisive victory. For nine years they had fought and died.

Now was a time of truce. But the Greeks were still dying. They were dying of a strange illness to which there was no known remedy. It was a clear sign of Apollo's wrath. But why such anger?

'Why?' asked Achilles, King of the Myrmidons, the strongest of all the warriors. 'Calchas, our priest and prophet, tell us the reason. Why does the god Apollo persecute us so? How have we offended him?'

Silence fell on the assembly of the Greek princes and Calchas, with a stern face and frowning forehead, replied, 'Apollo wants to punish he who holds as a slave the girl Chryseis, daughter of Chryses – the angered god's chosen priest. Chryses, you will remember, came here to ask for his daughter's release but met with a blunt refusal. For this Apollo strikes us.'

These words were greeted by a general whisper and all turned to Agamemnon, the supreme leader of the Greeks. It was he who held the lovely Chryseis as his slave, it therefore fell to him to placate Apollo's wrath by returning her to her father. But no one dared to speak. No one except Achilles who said, 'King, do what you must. Give up the girl.'

'Give her up?' asked Agamemnon haughtily, 'I, the leader? I can do, yes, but on one condition. In exchange for Chryseis, I want a slave as young and as beautiful as she. And I know just where to find one.'

'Perhaps you are thinking of Briseis, my own slave?' asked the troubled Achilles.

'Precisely,' came the harsh answer, 'and if you do not give her to me I shall take her myself!'

Achilles felt burning anger rise in his chest, and it was with great difficulty that he controlled himself and checked the impulse to reach for his sword. Trembling with rage he said, 'So that is your wish, is it? You want to take away from me

what I have fought for! The Trojans have never done me any harm, they have never offended me in any way, and yet I am fighting against them! And for whom? For you, you coward! I have left my country, I have come here and risked my life because a Trojan, Paris, has abducted Helen your brother's wife! You said the offence done to Menelaus was an offence to the whole of Greece, and we listened to you! We came to Troy and we have fought – and I, harder than anybody else! Is this to be my reward?'

In the frozen silence, Achilles went on, 'Beware Agamemnon, if you take Briseis away from me, I shall no longer fight. I shall sail back to Greece with my men!'

'Go, if you are afraid! We shall go on fighting without you!' Agamemnon cried.

For a moment it seemed that Achilles and Agamemnon were about to leap at each other's throats, but Nestor – the eldest and wisest of the Greeks – spoke up severely. 'Calm down both of you! Can't you see that you are only favouring the Trojans by behaving in this way? Agamemnon, you cannot take Briseis from Achilles and Achilles, you must have more respect for the king!'

These were wise words, but spoken in vain. Achilles contemptuously left the assembly and retired to his camp.

Soon afterwards two of Agamemnon's messengers arrived at his camp to fetch Briseis. Achilles raised no objection. He ordered Patroclus, his dearest and most loyal friend, 'Fetch the girl!'

Pale faced, Achilles watched Briseis as she was led away in tears.

A few days went by and a Greek ship entered the port of Chryse. Odysseus, King of Ithaca, stepped ashore and solemnly returned Chryseis to her father.

'Here is your daughter, Chryses – now ask Apollo to spare the Greeks!'

'I shall do so,' replied the priest. 'Come now, let us carry out the required sacrifices!'

Achilles watches the weeping Briseis as she is led away by Agamemnon's messengers

In the meantime, Achilles was beside himself with anger. His companions had never seen him so distraught. After a long outburst of bitter tears he paced along the shores of the crashing seas, trembling and cursing, and suddenly turned towards the sea and cried out, 'Mother! Mother! You who have brought me into this world – if only for a short while – hear me! They have offended me, they have humiliated me!'

He cried and sobbed again until out of the sea where she lived, rose Thetis, his divine mother, troubled to see her son in distress. She came to him and said, 'My child, why are you weeping?'

'You already know the reason, Mother. I beg of you, help me to seek revenge. You are a goddess, go to Zeus, father of all gods, and ask him to support the Trojans, to grant them victory so that the Greeks may see that without me, they have no hope of winning the war! Oh, Mother, I call upon you to hear me! Please help me!'

Moved, Thetis promised, and flew to Olympus, the sacred mountain where the gods assembled. She begged Zeus to help her avenge Achilles' honour and grief. Zeus, frowning, listened to her. The long war was worrying him and dividing all the gods. At last he answered, 'Thetis, I can refuse you nothing. So be it. The Greeks shall pay dearly for the injury they have inflicted upon your son!'

Looking out to sea, Achilles calls out to Thetis, his mother

9

Dream vanished and Agamemnon woke up, deeply impressed. So the gods had decided. He must attack and at once: victory was certain. He got dressed, buckled his sword belt and picked up his sceptre. He never imagined that by sending him Dream and inciting him to battle, Zeus intended to humiliate the Greeks, as he had promised his beloved Thetis. Agamemnon therefore summoned all the princes, and told them about his dream.

'Let us prepare,' he said, 'for the decisive battle. But first, in order to test our soldiers, I shall tell them that the war is over, that we have lost, that we shall never succeed in conquering Troy and that we must abandon our camp. When I have spoken, it will be your turn. Each one of you must speak out and urge his men to remain, exhort them to battle, remind them that the honour of Greece is at stake and that one cannot accept defeat. I am sure', he concluded, 'that this will inspire them to fight ardently and to win. I am certain that tomorrow, Troy shall be ours as I was told by the dream sent to me by Zeus himself.'

So a little while later the whole Greek army was gathered into a huge assembly. When Agamemnon appeared there was a great hush.

'Soldiers,' cried the king, 'nine years have now passed since we arrived on the shores of Troy. Nine years and we have not won. I confess that I have lost all hope of victory. Enough of war! Let us board our ships! Let us resign ourselves to defeat and return to Greece!'

There was a moment of utter silence amongst the soldiers, as though they could not believe what they had heard, then a mighty roar rose from the assembly.

BOOK II

It was night. All the men were asleep, so were all the gods – except Zeus. In his tent, Agamemnon was also asleep when descending swiftly from the heavens, Dream came silently to him and whispered in his ear, 'You sleep Agamemnon, even though you command an army and a fleet! Listen, Zeus has sent me. Through me he speaks. Do not hesitate any longer; gather your troops and move towards Troy. Fight and you shall win. Zeus and the other gods have decided so. Agamemnon, victory is yours. Take it!'

'Home! We are going home!' and they began to run towards the ships. In great confusion, tents were taken down, shelters dismantled, some men were already boarding ships whilst others were launching them out to sea. 'Greece! Greece! Home!'

Odysseus then stepped forward, ran to Agamemnon, snatched the sceptre from his hand and wielding it he addressed the most valiant of the leaders and soldiers.

'Have you gone mad!' he shouted. 'Where are you going? Where are you running to? Don't you understand that he, the powerful king, will punish you if you flee? Stop! Come back! The honour of Greece is at stake!'

At these words many stopped running and suddenly realized they had committed an act of cowardice. Many jumped off the ships and returned to the point of assembly. Among those who were set to go, Thersites – the ugliest and most evil of all the Greeks – shouted and protested louder than anybody else.

'What are you doing? Why are you stopping?' he shouted, running up and down. 'What do you care about Agamemnon and his brother Menelaus? What do you care about Helen's honour? Home, let's go home, and leave these worthless kings!'

Angered by these words, Odysseus struck at him with the sceptre and knocked him to the ground. The whimpering Thersites tried to protect himself from the blows and the soldiers around him laughed and sniggered and said, 'Odysseus has done some wonderful things in his life, but to shut Thersites' mouth is the most wonderful of all!'

Then Odysseus stood on the platform and addressed the warriors who had gathered around him. 'Greeks, it is true that we have been here for nine years, but it is all the more reason for us to hold on and fight till the end! What purpose will our efforts have served, why will our companions have died if we run away now? We will have failed in our word and disgraced our name! No, Agamemnon, we shall not leave you! Nobody,' he added, 'is thinking of returning home, not before we have taken Troy! Not before we have avenged Helen's honour, and the honour of Greece! But, he concluded threateningly, if any fool wants to leave, let him get to his ship, but let it be known that instead of escaping death he will meet with it instantly.'

From the platform Odysseus tells the soldiers to fight on to victory

The two entire armies on the battlefield, ready to confront each other

In the silence, Agamemnon stepped forward. 'In the name of Greece, my friends, let us then prepare for the decisive battle! Yes, victory is ours! Eat now, then sharpen all swords and spears, and let each man join his rank, his companions and his prince. We shall attack and we shall not stop fighting until we are inside Troy!'

A great cheer acclaimed these words, and a few hours later the Greeks moved in battle order towards the city. Those who were able to, had made offerings to the gods and prayed that they might be saved from death. But they were all determined to fight and put an end to the war which had lasted too long. In a clatter of iron, the Greek army marched to battle, across the vast green plain which lay before Troy, and where ran the rivers Simoenta and Scamander (which the gods also called Xanthus).

Meanwhile in Troy, a conference was taking place. The Trojans had gathered around their wise old King Priam and were discussing the war and what could be done to end it. The discussion was suddenly interrupted by a sentry who rushed in from the walls. 'Kings! Brothers!' he shouted, 'The Greeks are coming!'

Instantly Hector, the Trojan leader, son of Priam, leapt to his feet and exclaimed, 'To your posts! The meeting is adjourned! Be ready to leave the city!' Immediately, they all rushed to arm themselves, while the elderly, the women and the children anxiously gathered on the walls.

The trumpets blared, the horses pawed the ground, the ranks fell into line and the gates were flung open, for Hector wanted to face the enemy on the open field. One by one the bristling divisions marched out and lined up for battle around Thorn Hill – a lonely hillock which stood out in the middle of the plain. The two entire armies were on the field facing each other. Such an array of forces had never been seen. The battle which was about to begin was perhaps to decide the fate of the war.

However, among the princes, one leader was missing. Achilles, the most feared Greek and the bravest, had remained in his tent.

BOOK III

As the two armies drew nearer to each other, Priam ordered Helen to meet him on the walls.

'You sent for me?' asked the beautiful woman for whom so much blood had been shed. 'What is it you wish, O Father and King?'

'I want you to show me one by one who the Greek leaders are. Who is that man with the shining armour who walks ahead of them all?'

'That is Agamemnon, my brother-in-law and overlord of the Greeks.'

'And those two men who lead such compact divisions, who are they? One is as tall as a giant, the other is shorter but broader in the shoulders.'

'The first one is the very powerful and most valiant Telamonian Aias. The other is Odysseus, King of Ithaca.'

From the walls of Troy, Priam and Helen watch the Greek army

Paris and Menelaus challenge each other to a duel to decide the fate of the war

'And that one, so noble and proud?' asked Priam again.

Troubled, Helen replied, 'That is Menelaus, my husband, from whom your son Paris abducted me.'

At that moment, Paris himself stepped forward from the Trojan ranks. Paris who had caused the war by abducting Helen, was very handsome in his flashing armour. He looked at the Greeks with arrogance, as though he wanted to defy them all. But when amongst them he noticed the tall figure of Menelaus, all his boldness disappeared. He halted, lowered his spear and meekly turned round to join his companions.

Hector, who had noticed all this, exclaimed with contempt, 'Paris! Aren't you ashamed of yourself? You walked high and mighty ahead of everyone, you seemed ready to take on the whole

Greek army by yourself, but when you saw Menelaus, your knees faltered and your heart quivered. Yet it is for you that we are fighting, don't you forget it!'

Hurt by these harsh words Paris replied, 'No, Brother! I shan't forget it. I admit I was frightened but it was only a fleeting moment of weakness. Listen to me: I shall go and challenge Menelaus to a duel. He and I alone will fight and so we shall decide the fate of the war. If he wins, return Helen to him and let the war be over. If I win, the Greeks must leave.'

Hector then ordered everyone to halt. In a clatter of arms and rising clouds of dust, the Trojans stopped, keeping in battle ranks. The Greeks also came to a halt. Agamemnon stepped forward on his own and shouted, 'Hector, what do you want? Why have you stopped? Do you want to surrender?'

14

'That you can never hope for, Agamemnon!' replied Hector, 'Paris is challenging your brother Menelaus to single combat! Greece on one side Troy on the other. The winner will decide the outcome of the war. Do you agree?'

Agamemnon agreed. And while the two armies stood motionless and silent in their ranks, Paris and Menelaus advanced towards each other. The Trojan war could well have ended there and then. Wielding their spears, the two men confronted each other. The first to strike was Paris. He threw his lance which whistled towards his opponent. Menelaus raised his shield and warded off the blow. Then in his turn, he launched his spear and struck his enemy's shield. At the same time, they both unsheathed their swords and went for each other. In the breathless silence only the clanging of the blades was heard. Paris was the younger and stronger of the two, but he was not as brave as Menelaus whose thirst for revenge swelled his heart and increased his strength. Menelaus struck with such fury that his sword shattered against Paris' shield.

A whisper rose from the spectators. Menelaus was disarmed, Paris could easily kill him. No. Before the young Trojan could move forward and strike, Menelaus lunged at him with his bare hands, caught him by his helmet and tugged at it with all his might. Paris tried to react but the strap was strangling him, the sword dropped from his hand, Menelaus pulled again and again till the strap broke and the Greek fell to the ground with the empty helmet in his arms. He jumped back to his feet, picked up his spear and with a cry leapt forward to stab his hated rival . . . but he was no longer there. Paris had vanished.

Aphrodite, the goddess of love, who had always protected the young Trojan prince, had protected him once more at this critical moment. She had surrounded him with a cloud of dust and had carried him off. Menelaus' spear sank into the ground.

Yet there was no doubt. The winner was the Greek. The Trojans could see that and withdrew in silence. Then Agamemnon moved forward and shouted, 'Greeks! Trojans! Hear me. You have all witnessed Menelaus' victory! According to our agreement Hector must return Helen to us, and may there now be peace!'

15

The gods meet to discuss Troy's destiny

BOOK IV

Whilst all this was taking place on the plain, the gods were once more conferring on Mount Olympus. Frowning, Zeus said, 'Athene and Hera to be sure, are on Menelaus' side, but they are content to watch and smile upon him. Whereas you Aphrodite, you descended to save Paris although he had been defeated and therefore deserved to perish. I am tired of this war. Let us put an end to it. Let us return Helen to Menelaus and let it be over!'

To this Hera replied, 'No, I don't want to see peace restored until Troy is destroyed!'

'What harm have Priam and his sons caused you that you want to see them all destroyed? Beware, Hera, if you want Troy to perish, perhaps one day I shall wipe out a city that is dear to you!'

'So be it! If that is your wish,' exclaimed the angry goddess. 'You can even destroy Athens or Sparta or Argos, my beloved cities. I shall not oppose your will, but do not oppose mine. Right now let them break the truce and resume combat. Athene it is up to you. Think of something! I want to see Troy destroyed.'

Athene swiftly left Olympus and descended to earth only a moment after Agamemnon had asked Hector to keep to the agreement. Assuming the appearance of a Trojan warrior, Laodocus, the goddess, came up to Pandarus, a very skilled archer who seldom missed his aim, and whispered to him, 'Pandarus, do not hesitate. If you love Troy, if you want to be honoured, if you want to win this war by yourself, then shoot! The time is right. Look, there is Menelaus still on his own where the duel took place. Kill him with an arrow. You can do it and you shall reap glory from it! The war is over! Do not hesitate!'

Pandarus was a man of honour and courage but Athene's words impressed and influenced him. Yes, the pacts had been solemnly drawn between Agamemnon and Hector but it would be worthwhile to break them if, with one arrow only, the war could be stopped and Troy saved.

Unseen, Pandarus notched a long arrow to his mighty bow, took aim, drew back the string, released it ... The arrow was sent whistling through the air and would have pierced Menelaus' heart had not Athene – as quick as lightning – diverted it. The arrow hit the prince on his side, through the studded armour, cut the leather belt and sank into the flesh. Menelaus let out a brief cry and fell to his knees. Already the blood was spilling on to the earth. In a great uproar of fury and indignation the Greeks drew together brandishing their weapons.

'Treason! Treason!' they shouted, as Agamemnon bent over his brother lying on the ground.

'Fetch Machaon the doctor, tell him to be quick! In the meantime let us prepare! The Trojans will pay for this! No, brother,' he added seeing that Menelaus tried to pull out the arrow from his side, 'let Machaon tend to it. You shall not die from this wound and you shall fight again!'

Pandarus hits Menelaus with an arrow and so breaks the peace treaty

17

The other Greek princes rushed about while the whole army moved threateningly. The battle was about to start.

Meanwhile, a herald had hurriedly gone to fetch Machaon, son of Asclepius, the great physician. 'Come quickly,' he said, 'Menelaus has been wounded by an arrow. You must save him!'

Machaon tends the wounded Menelaus

Machaon hastened to the field where Menelaus lay, blood streaming from his wound. His friends had gathered close around him to protect and comfort him. Making his way through them, Machaon bent down, took a firm hold of the arrow and with a resolute pull removed it from the flesh.

'Do not fear, Menelaus,' he said, 'the wound is not as deep as you think.' Then he removed the prince's belt and armour, 'I can now dress your wound.'

'The enemy is coming!' someone shouted suddenly.

Indeed the Trojans, led by Hector, were advancing ready for the attack. Recovering from their bewilderment, the Trojans had reorganized their ranks for battle. They had hoped of course that the war would have been over with the outcome of the duel between Paris and Menelaus. Not everyone approved of Pandarus' action! But since the arrow had been shot and the blood had been shed and the peace treaty violated, it was clear that they must fight again. And fight they would for Troy must be defended at all cost, and although Paris was a cowardly warrior, it was worth fighting for a woman as beautiful as Helen.

'Forward, my friends!' Hector called out brandishing his sword. 'Our destiny lies in the battle!'

Hearing this Agamemnon unsheathed his shining sword and left Menelaus in the care of Machaon.

'Let the Trojans come, then! It is certainly not to the Trojans, who break peace treaties, that Zeus will lend his help!' he shouted. Before mounting his war chariot to which were harnessed two splendid, restless horses, the king passed his troops in review and addressed them thus: 'The time has come, sons of Greece! Here our fate will be decided! If we win we shall enter Troy, if we lose, the enemy will reach our camp, set fire to our ships and we shall lose all hope of sailing back to our country.'

'Odysseus, I am relying on you! Idomeneus, King of Crete, be strong in battle! Aias, son of Oïleus,' Agamemnon went on, 'Telamonian Aias, heroes, if I had more leaders as worthy as you the war would have been over long ago! Nestor, my friend, fight by my side! Diomedes, stand high on your chariot and strike boldly! Greeks, let's go! To battle!'

BOOK V

The two armies drew up opposite each other, led by the leaders standing tall on their chariots. As they marched the warriors shouted and shook their spears. Their shields glistened in the sun and the clang of arms rose to the sky. Even before the two armies met, showers of arrows rained down from the opposing ranks and some soldiers fell dead or wounded. But that did not stop the others. Like the wind-blown waves of the sea that come crashing down on the reef, retreating and surging forward with a mighty roar, so clashed the ranks of the Greeks and the Trojans. The latter had Athene against them and they knew it, but they also knew that Ares, the god of war, was on their side. In fact the gods, having come down from Olympus, took part in the battle, some to kill or spread terror, others to spare a life or give comfort to a dying man. Indeed, many of the warriors had a god as a mother or father. This was a war fought as much in heaven as on the plain which stretched out from the great walls of Troy and down to the sea.

Shields clashed against one another, spears crossed, iron-clad and leather-belted men came to blows, the air which had so-far echoed with shouts and insults, was now filled with moans and cries of lamentation, triumph or challenge. Voices of those dying and those killing, of the victors and of the defeated, mingled together. The first to fall was Phegeus, son of Dares, a young Trojan who was speared in the chest by Diomedes. Phegeus fell amidst a frightful clatter of bronze. Around his body the fury of the fight immediately intensified, because in this war, the dead were stripped of their weapons and it was a bitter disgrace to leave the corpse of a companion in the hands of the enemy.

It would be too lengthy to list all the princes, warriors or simple soldiers who met with death in that battle. It seemed that, after the first encounter, the Trojans were about to retreat under the enemy's assault, when Apollo's voice was heard above the din of the battle. 'Trojans, do not retreat! What do you fear? The flesh of the Greeks is not made of stone or iron that it cannot be wounded! Remember that today Achilles is not fighting! Forward! Forward!'

The Trojans counter-attacked and in the blood and the dust, the stamping of the horses and the squeaking of the chariots, under the rain of arrows and spears, there was Ares on the one side and Athene on the other jeering at each other. Weary, Athene suddenly called out, 'Ares, you who slaughter men in battle, come with me! Let us retire from the struggle, let us fight no more! Let us not anger our father, Zeus!' Thus speaking she took her violent brother by the hand and led him to the shore of the Scamander river. There they both came to a halt, panting and stained with blood.

The battle, though, continued to rage. Diomedes, one of the most valiant Greek princes, carried away with heroism flung himself on the Trojans with increasing fierceness, who, under his savage blows were again forced to draw back. Diomedes was like a stream in full spate, destroying everything and impossible to contain. But Pandarus, the same man who a little while ago had so treacherously wounded Menelaus, did not flinch at the sight of Diomedes. He notched an arrow to his mighty bow and did not miss his shot. The arrow struck Diomedes in the shoulder and he stopped and fell to his knees. A cheer of triumph rose and the Trojans resumed their attack. But the indomitable Diomedes fought back the pain and the weakness.

'Sthenelus', he ordered a companion, 'pull the arrow from my wound so that I may return to battle! And you Athene, give me back my strength and let me kill the man who has struck me!' The arrow was torn away and although he was losing blood, Diomedes went back into battle.

The field was red with blood and cluttered with fallen warriors. Two of Priam's sons, Chromius and Echemmon, who fought together in the same chariot were met by the enraged Diomedes. They were struck down, killed and stripped of their armour.

Then Aeneas, King of the Dardans and son of Aphrodite, summoned Pandarus. 'Pandarus,' he called out, 'we must stop Diomedes! Get on my chariot and let us away!'

Pandarus called as he came running, 'I have already struck the butcher now I shall kill him!

You drive the chariot, I'll take the spear.' They steered frantically across the battlefield in Diomedes' direction.

Sthenelus saw them coming and warned, 'Diomedes, fall back! Aeneas and Pandarus are coming for you! You are wounded, do not expose yourself!' Diomedes took no heed and fearlessly stood firm so that when Pandarus hurled the spear at him with all his might, he was ready to ward off the blow.

'He missed!' shouted Diomedes who retaliated with his spear. It stuck Pandarus through the throat and he fell dead from the chariot. Aeneas was ready to defend his friend's body, but Diomedes picked up a huge rock and hurled it at him, crushing his leg. Aeneas sank to his knees and would certainly have died by the bloody spear of his enemy, had not Aphrodite come to his rescue, hiding him under a fold of her veil. But not even a goddess could stop Diomedes, who shouting, ran in hot pursuit of Aphrodite and cut her wrist with his spear.

The beautiful goddess screamed with pain and the warrior bawled, 'Off with you! This is war and if you wanted to see what it was like, now you know!'

In a whirlwind, Aphrodite returned to Olympus weeping. She was shaken and bloodstained but she had saved her beloved son Aeneas from certain death.

Diomedes strength came from Athene who, after getting her breath back, had gone once more into the battle. Immediately, Ares had followed her, rushing to the aid of the Trojans.

'How much longer will you allow this massacre to continue?' he called out to them. 'Aeneas is wounded. Perhaps you want to leave him in the hands of the enemy?'

Roused by these words, the Trojans made a desperate counter-attack. Hector led on his chariot, opening their way into the enemy until he reached Aeneas and snatched him from the Greeks. Although in a sorry state, Aeneas was still able to fight. But once again the Trojans

The battle between Trojans and Greeks rages on furiously

were compelled to retreat and found themselves driven back under the walls of Troy.

One of Priam's sons, the valiant Helenus, who had fought all day on the frontline, approached Hector and said, 'Brother, things are getting bad. We have not yet lost but the gates of Troy are so close that someone might be tempted to take refuge inside the city – and that would be a disaster. You and Aeneas must tell the men to carry on fighting and they will fight. But Hector, this is not enough. You must go into the city and ask the older women to make an offering to Athene of a robe, the loveliest they can find. She must cease to be our enemy!'

Hector assented and with Aeneas by his side he rode to the frontline, rousing his men's fighting spirit and urging them to resist. Then he rushed inside the city of Troy through a door that was opened for him.

Hecuba and the Trojan ladies make an offering to Athene of their most precious robe

BOOK VI

Bloodstained, covered in dust and drenched in perspiration under his dented armour, Hector reached Priam's royal palace. He was climbing up the stairs when Hecuba his mother, came rushing to him.

'Hector, my son, have you come to pray to Zeus so that he will support us in battle? Yes, you must! But first drink this wine, it will refresh you. You are tired, I can see it!'

'No, noble mother, do not offer me wine. I dare not drink to Zeus with my hands covered in blood. And wine robs a man of his strength. But listen to me. Collect your daughters, your daughters-in-law and the noble ladies of Troy and take your most precious robe to Athene as a gift.

Promise her that every year we shall sacrifice to her twelve of the best cows in the land. Pray she may keep Diomedes away from battle. He is the one who is destroying us! Do it now, Mother! I am going to look for Paris!'

Having spoken, Hector hastened through the corridors and the splendid rooms of the palace. Shortly after, Hecuba together with the other women, solemnly laid before Athene's statue, the most richly embroidered robe she possessed. She promised the wrathful goddess numerous and generous sacrifices.

'O, Goddess,' prayed the Trojan women, 'break the spear of Diomedes, the slaughterer.' But it was to no avail; Athene shook her head.

Meanwhile Hector reached Helen's quarters. There he found Paris sitting peacefully by his beautiful wife, quietly polishing his helmet, armour and shield.

'Shame on you!' Hector shouted reproachfully. 'Our men are falling all around the city because of you, and what do you do? You polish these weapons you don't even have the courage to use! Off with you, rascal, run to your post and fight!'

'Hector, my brother,' replied Paris blushing, 'yes you are right, you all fight and I remain inside, but be patient, try to understand me. I was only seeking comfort at Helen's side. Anyway she has urged me to return to the front. I shall only be a moment, then I shall put on my armour and join you!'

Then Helen spoke. 'Hector, I would rather be dead than be the cause of this war! I have tried to convince Paris to fight, but his heart is what it is! Come and sit by me, brother-in-law, rest awhile and ...'

Hector reproaches Paris, who instead of fighting, idles by Helen's side

Hector takes Astyanax in his arms and prays to the gods to make him strong

'I cannot Helen!' interrupted Hector. 'The Trojans are struggling and they need me. I wish to see my wife and son. You see to it that Paris gets ready and goes back to his post. This is a decisive day which might bring the end of us!' And Hector left to find his wife, Andromache.

But she was not in her rooms, nor with Hecuba and the other women making the offerings to Athene's statue. Having heard that the Greeks were winning, she had taken with her a maid and her little son Astyanax and had rushed to the walls and climbed up the tower over the Scaean Gate which overlooked the battlefield. So to the Scaean gate Hector hastened. When Andromache saw him, she ran into his arms, pale and distraught.

As Hector looked at Astyanax and smiled, she whispered, 'Ah, you unfortunate man! This bravery of yours will be the end of you! Have you no pity for me, Hector, nor for your little son? I have nobody else in the world but you. You are to me a husband, father, mother and brother. Have mercy on us, stay here in the tower! Rally the army from inside the city without going out to battle!'

'I should like to, wife,' replied Hector thoughtfully, 'but I cannot fail in my duty. Perhaps I shall die, but at least you will be proud to have been the wife of a fighter who did not take flight.' Then he added softly, 'Give me the child!' He took Astyanax in his arms, who terrified by his father's countenance and his helmet let out a childish wail.

The hero smiled and took his helmet off. He kissed his son and said, 'Zeus and you other gods, grant me that this boy of mine may grow strong and reign over Troy. Many people say he is stronger than his father!'

Then handing the boy back to his wife, he went on, 'Do not weep Andromache. If my fate is to live no one can kill me. But death awaits us all, cowards and heroes alike and no one can escape it. Be brave!' As he spoke he put on his helmet and left the fair Andromache in tears. He came down from the tower and headed for the gate. On his way he met Paris dressed for battle, and together they rejoined their army.

BOOK VII

As soon as both men had resumed their posts, the Trojans took courage and pressed forward. At their unexpected counter-attack the Greeks drew back. From the heights of Mount Olympus where the weary Athene had retired, she saw what was happening. She swiftly took off for Troy and had barely set foot on earth when she met Apollo.

'Athene, why have you flown down from Olympus once again? Are you keen to see Troy sacked? Listen to me: too much blood has been shed. Let us unite and put an end to this massacre. They will fight again to be sure, but it is enough for today.'

'Yes, Apollo,' replied the goddess, 'I also feel that it is enough for today. But how can we stop the men fighting?'

'There is a way. Let us make Hector challenge one of the Greek princes to a duel. That way the battle will cease.'

Athene and Apollo talk of a way to stop the fighting

25

The two children of Zeus agreed and induced Helenus to speak the following words to his brother Hector, 'Hear me, Hector, I don't know what has come over me but I feel certain that you shall not die today. Have our men sit down and order them to stop fighting. Then go forward alone and challenge a Greek to a duel.'

Hector agreed. Pacing up and down in front of his troops he commanded the men to cease fighting and sit down on the ground. Seeing the Trojans laying down their arms and sit in orderly ranks, Agamemnon immediately gave the same order to the Greeks. A great silence fell where only a short while earlier battle had raged. Everyone was now still where before there had been a frenzied turmoil of men and chariots. Hector stepped forward and stood between the two armies.

'Hear me all! The outcome of this war is victory or death. I am here to challenge any Greek who is prepared to fight me! This is my proposal and may Zeus be my witness. The victor will strip the other of his arms but must send the corpse back so that he may be given a warrior's burial. Come now! Who will accept my challenge?'

A long silence followed these words. Hector was a great warrior and he fought to defend his country. No Greek was then willing to take up such a challenge.

The long embarassed silence lasted till old Nestor exclaimed, 'Oh, shame on you Greeks. Can it be that not one of you will step forward? If I were young, I would take on Hector!'

At the old man's words nine Greek princes stood up, their faces red with shame. They were

Hector orders the fighting to stop and challenges the Greeks to a duel

Hector and Aias Telamonian draw their swords and fight against each other

Agamemnon, Diomedes, Aias (son of Oïleus), Telamonian Aias, Idomeneus, Meriones, Odysseus, Eurypylus and Thoas; all ready for the duel. A draw was to pick Hector's opponent. Fate chose Telamonian Aias, the tallest and strongest of the Greeks. When Hector saw him advancing, clad in bronze with his vast shield, wielding his spear and with a threatening sneer on his face, he felt nervous. But to have withdrawn then would have meant eternal shame for him. So he stood firm and waited.

'Hector,' shouted Aias, stopping at some distance, 'you see that although Achilles is not amongst us today, we can still fight. You go first and begin the duel.'

'So be it Aias and let it be an open fight!' As he spoke Hector launched his spear which planted itself into Aias' shield with a heavy thud. Aias retaliated by piercing Hector's shield with his spear. Having no more spears, the two heroes began to hurl great boulders at each other.

Struck and wounded in the neck, Hector staggered to his knees, but Apollo quickly helped him up again. Drawing their swords, the rivals closed in on each other and would have fought relentlessly until death, had not two heralds, a Greek and a Trojan, come up and separated them.

'Enough, valiant warriors,' they said, 'Stop the fighting. You are both brave and both loved by Zeus. Enough, it is nearly dark!'

'So be it Aias!' said Hector. 'We have struck each other many blows, let us now exchange gifts so that it may be said by all, these two have fought each other fiercely but they have parted friends!' With this he handed his opponent his sword and received Aias' valuable purple belt. So ended the duel.

There was no more fighting on that day. The remaining hours before sunset were devoted to the sad task of gathering and burying with all the honours the warriors who had fallen in combat.

BOOK VIII

Another day began. On Mount Olympus, Zeus summoned all the gods to a conference. His face was sombre. 'Listen to me all, and listen well. I shall tell you what I think and let none of you contradict me. What is happening in Troy is worrying and annoying me. It must end. I won't have any of you going down to help either the Greeks or the Trojans. I have spoken many times before but you have taken no notice. Well, if I see any one of you, whoever it is, flying down to earth to meddle in this wretched war, I shall strike him with my lightning. Then you will know the wrath of Zeus.'

With this, Zeus mounted his chariot and flew off to Mount Ida from where he could survey the battlefield. Impressed, the gods dared not move and remained on Olympus, silent and thoughtful.

Meanwhile, at sunrise, Greeks and Trojans had taken up their arms again and were preparing for another battle. Soon the converging forces met and the same bloody scenes repeated themselves. More dead, more suffering, more heroes fell to the ground and were stripped of their arms. The fight lasted through the morning, until at last Zeus brought out the Scales of Fortune. He placed the Greeks' fate on one plate and the Trojans' fate on the other. The latter felt heavier which meant that Fortune was on the Trojans' side.

Zeus immediately sent a flash of lightning down among the Greek troops, who, terrified by the deafening blast, scattered in all directions with the enemy following at their heels. During the retreat, old Nestor alone lingered behind, and would have been easy prey for the Trojans but for Diomedes, who noticed him. He steered his chariot round and whipping the horses furiously drove to his rescue.

On his chariot, Zeus goes to Mount Ida to watch the battlefield

Zeus sends a bolt of lightning to earth which falls in front of Diomedes' chariot

'Where are you running to, Greeks?' he shouted as he rode. 'Are you fleeing too Odysseus? Won't you come and help me to rescue Nestor?' His words were lost in the turmoil and alone, he drew up to the old man, lept off the chariot and helped Nestor on to it.

'We shall not flee, Nestor,' he said. 'Though you are old I shall take you to battle and Hector will see who we are. Sthenelus!' he ordered his faithful charioteer, 'Head straight for Hector!'

So in the general flight, Diomedes returned alone to the attack, aiming his spear at Hector's heart. He missed but instead struck the Trojan hero's charioteer. Zeus then intervened once more and with a terrific thunderclap he flashed a dazzling bolt to earth, right in front of Diomedes' chariot. The frightened horses neighed and reared, and Nestor shouted, 'Ah! Diomedes! I fear this is a sign from the gods! Zeus is against us! Let us withdraw!'

'I shall not withdraw! Let no one say that I was afraid!'

'Indeed, no one who knows you shall ever dare to say that, Diomedes,' replied Nestor worriedly. 'But do not defy the wrath of Zeus again!'

Finally the chariot was steered round in the dust and driven back to the Greek camp, while the Trojans, taking courage, pressed forward with a terrific roar, led by Hector who urged them from his chariot.

'Trojans, allies, friends! Yesterday Fortune was not on our side but today we shall win! If our fighting spirit holds, today we shall invade the Greek camp and end the war! Go! Do not linger! As Diomedes flees we shall go after him! Forward!'

They all followed him and not one Greek warrior dared to turn round and face them. It was indeed a terrible downfall. Never had the Greeks fled in this manner before. One by one or in disorderly groups they scrambled across the trench which protected their camp and took refuge behind the wall that surrounded it. The Trojans kept at their heels relentlessly, bombarding them with arrows and spears. In short, not one Greek remained outside the wall.

It was a strong and well-built wall with solid ramparts that protected the Greek camp, the tents, the headquarters and the ships which were nearly all dry-docked along the shore. The ships were for the Greeks an indispensable element in the war, because if they were lost they could not get weapon and war supply reinforcements. But losing the ships would mean an even greater disaster: without the ships how could they sail back to their homeland?

Intent as they were to reach the wall, the Trojans hadn't looked at the sky, they hadn't realized that the sun had completed its course and was setting. When the shadows of night fell with a long gust of wind, Hector was taken aback and shocked. He turned to the sea reddened by sunset. Stopping in his tracks, he halted his troops and shouted, 'Enough, brothers! Stop here! I hoped to assail the enemy ships but soon it will be dark. We must respect the night and stop fighting! It does not matter,' he added, 'this time we shall not withdraw, we shall not return to the city, we shall not leave this ground that we have conquered. Send a messenger to tell our wives and friends that the army will stay on the field. The Greeks,' he went on, pointing at the wall, 'cannot escape us. Tomorrow at dawn we shall break through their defences and set fire to their ships. When they have lost their means of retreat they will also lose heart to fight. You will see! Nobody in the world will ever dare to make war on Troy! Let us pitch camp and light huge fires. From those fires we shall take the flames which tomorrow will burn down the enemy ships!'

Hector orders his men to pitch camp and light fires. They will spend the night on conquered land instead of going back to the city

Nestor reproaches Agamemnon for having quarrelled with Achilles

BOOK IX

Inside their camp that night, the Greeks could not sleep as they were worried. The sentries paced the ramparts, silently watching the fires as they were lit by the Trojans, and listening to their songs of victory.

The Greek princes were holding a meeting in Agamemnon's tent. Never in nine years of war had they suffered such a bitter defeat. 'I had not suspected such fighting fury from the Trojans,' mumbled Agamemnon disheartened. 'I really didn't know they had it in them. It must be a sign from the heavens. Zeus is telling us that we shall never take Troy!'

'Do not speak so! We shall take Troy even if I must do it alone with my charioteer Sthenelus!' replied Diomedes harshly.

Old Nestor intervened, 'It is not with words that one fights. Agamemnon you are discouraged and it is understandable, but remember we are battling without Achilles, and without his mighty arm – like it or not – we cannot hope to win. I shall be frank with you, you have offended him, it is now up to you to make peace with him.'

After a moment of silence Agamemnon whispered, 'Yes, I admit I have offended Achilles. He has refused to fight and that is the cause of our

31

In his tent, Achilles plays the lyre while Patroclus listens silently

defeat. Friends,' he went on, 'I know I was wrong, but I am your king and leader. Hear then what I have to say to you and I hope that by tomorrow Achilles will go back to battle.'

Soon after, Nestor, Aias and Odysseus left Agamemnon's tent and walking along the seashore headed towards Achilles' campsite, well guarded by the Myrmidons of the long spears.

Achilles was in his tent with his good friend Patroclus. They were unarmed and their armour, shields, leggings and helmets stood in a corner of the tent. Sitting on a bench, Achilles was playing his lyre, humming ancient songs which told of war and heroic feats, while Patroclus listened in silence. It was as though they were a thousand miles away from Troy and the bloody battlefield, but in Achilles' heart anger and contempt still burnt.

At the sight of Nestor, Aias and Odysseus, the young man at once put down his lyre, stood to his feet with a smile and stretched out his arms.

'Friends!' he exclaimed, 'What a joy it is to see you again! Come! And you Patroclus, pour us some of the reddest and purest wine! Odysseus, Aias, wise Nestor! Drink and eat with me!'

And so they ate and drank and talked as though nothing had happened in the past few days. At last raising his cup to Achilles, Odysseus said, 'Friend, it is not only to drink that we have come. We have just been holding a conference in Agamemnon's tent. Achilles, glory of all Greece, Agamemnon has sent us to tell you that he admits to his error, he admits that he has offended you by taking away Briseis from you, whom you had well deserved by your courage. If you will go back to battle he is ready to return her to you. Not only that but when Troy is sacked you will have the privilege of choosing twenty slaves from among the most beautiful Trojan maidens and when we sail back to Greece you may marry one of Agamemnon's daughters. You will be Achilles, son-in-law of the king of all Greeks. This we have come to tell you. We are asking you to fight again.'

Odysseus had spoken. He was now quiet. A long silence followed and Achilles replied in a low tone, 'Odysseus you have been frank with me, so I shall be frank with you. You have been sent by the man I hate more than anyone in the world. He had my trust, he has lost it. He had my friendship, he has lost it. He has shown that he possessed neither generosity nor loyalty. I have served him faithfully and as a reward he has taken away my precious Briseis, the girl whom I loved. Agamemnon will never be able to convince me of his change of heart. He sent you to me not because he has understood that he was unfair, but only because he has suffered a bitter defeat on the battleground. Let him fight on alone against Hector. Anyway,' the young man went on, 'I shall soon be off, I shall soon be leaving this land where I certainly never came of my own free will!'

'Achilles …' Odysseus began to say, but Achilles continued, 'My mother Thetis, hearing that I was leaving for Troy, told me that by coming here to fight I would find death and with it eternal glory, and she added that if I did not take part in the war, my life would instead be a long and happy one. Well I have changed my mind. I now choose a long and happy life and I advise you all to do the same. It is useless to carry on. You will never conquer Troy.'

An astounded silence followed these words. Odysseus and his companions tried in vain to convince Achilles to change his mind. So after they had drunk a last cup of wine, the three of them went back to Agamemnon with the bitter answer. Achilles was not giving in, he was still angered. He would not return to fight.

Achilles does not give in to Nestor's plea and refuses to return to battle

33

Odysseus and Diomedes meet Dolon on his way to spy on their camp

BOOK X

In the still of night the soldiers exhausted by their day of fighting had laid down on the ground to rest and sleep. But not all were asleep. Anxiety kept Agamemnon awake. The Trojans had stirred along the wall not far from the ships. What were they up to? They would surely attack, but when? Tonight? Tomorrow?

Never had Hector come so close. With a sombre face Agamemnon watched the many fires the Trojans had lit on the plain. The danger was great and the Greeks might well be doomed to disaster.

At last the king came to a decision. He could no longer contain his anguish and so went to each of the leaders' tents and called them out one by one for yet another war meeting.

'It is necessary,' he began, 'to know what the Trojans' intentions are, whether they will attack tonight or wait until tomorrow. Our troops are tired and most of them are asleep. We must know if we can let them sleep or if we must line them up for battle.'

Odysseus and Diomedes volunteered to go and spy on the Trojans. Stealthily they crept out through a small door in the wall and walking silently across the plain littered with corpses and weapons, they came close to the enemy fires. Suddenly Odysseus held back his companion, and whispered, 'Stop! I think I can hear someone coming.'

He was right, a shadow appeared out of the darkness and they saw the glint of armour. Diomedes leapt forward brandishing his spear. 'Stop!' he shouted. 'Who goes there?'

The man stopped and fearfully implored, 'Don't harm me, spare me!'

'Who are you? Speak up if you don't want to die where you stand!'

'My name is Dolon. Hector sent me. I was told to creep into your camp,' replied the man with a trembling voice. 'To find out what you were doing, whether you were going to fight again or were preparing to leave.'

'Ah! So you think you have defeated us once and for all? No, Dolon we are not leaving. But speak up, have you perhaps received reinforcements to feel so sure of yourselves?'

Dolon, who had accepted the spying mission to the Greek camp only because he had been offered a handsome reward, replied, 'Yes. The Thracians have come led by their young King Rhesus. They are camping over there on the right. Rhesus,' he added, 'owns two beautiful white horses, the loveliest I have ever seen. But please let me go, I ...' He was not able to finish his sentence, Diomedes had struck him a fatal blow with his sword. 'If that one had reported back to Hector, we would have been done for,' he explained. 'But come Odysseus let us bid welcome to the Thracians!'

They walked on and reached the Trojan camp. Some soldiers were armed, others were asleep. The two heroes slipped unseen and noiselessly towards the still tents and headed for the enclosure where several horses slept. Yes, Dolon had spoken the truth. The two big thoroughbreds were certainly the most handsome creatures ever seen under the walls of Troy! Ah, if only they could take them back to their camp as loot, what a boast it would be!

'I'll take care of the beasts,' whispered Odysseus, 'you take care of the men.'

Diomedes nodded and moved stealthily towards a huge tent. Meanwhile, Odysseus, crawling on the ground, reached the enclosure and found a way in. He moved slowly and cautiously among the horses so that they wouldn't feel his presence and start to paw and whinny. He had reached the splendid white horses that belonged to King Rhesus!

Odysseus takes hold of Rhesus' two splendid white horses

At that moment Diomedes had penetrated the Thracian quarters. As soon as they had arrived, the Thracians had retired to bed in order to be fresh for the next day's battle. It was indeed ill luck to have joined at a moment of victory. Ill luck because feeling very bold and sure of themselves they had not even remembered to put out sentries to watch over the camp.

The terrible Diomedes unsheathed his sword and, since in times of war any action which can harm the enemy and undermine his strength is fully justified, one by one he killed at least twelve warriors in their sleep – among whom was the young King Rhesus, who had come to Troy hoping to find glory and was instead slaughtered like a lamb. Diomedes would have continued his massacre had he not feared someone might wake up and raise the alarm. Thinking that Odysseus had already got hold of the horses, he decided to return, his sword still dripping with blood. Odysseus was waiting impatiently for him to return.

'Quick! The Trojans are everywhere! If they find us, all is lost!'

'At least twelve of them, and Rhesus among them, will never find out anything,' replied Diomedes with a sneer. 'Come, let's take the chariot and leave!'

They harnessed the two horses to Rhesus' chariot, lashed the animals on and made their way back to the Greek camp. Their screams and the noise of the hooves woke the Thracian soldiers who discovered the men slaughtered in their sleep. The alarm was promptly raised and all the Trojan princes and Hector came running. Alas, it was too late; Rhesus lay dead in a pool of his own blood, and the cloud of dust visible in the night showed that his murderers were in full flight taking with them the two splendid horses.

Such was war. They weep on one side, they rejoice on the other. So the Trojan camp was in mourning whilst the Greeks celebrated Odysseus' and Diomedes' mission with wine and song.

After having harnessed the two horses to Rhesus' chariot, Odysseus and Diomedes head back to camp

BOOK XI

At last dawn broke. Their strength restored by night, the Greeks prepared to counter-attack. They must drive back the enemy as far as possible away from the ships. Therefore they must leave the camp in force to go to battle.

As on the previous day and many other times during the nine long years, the troops in battle array, clashed. Once more chariots were driven furiously at soldiers, once more brave young men challenged each other, met in combat, killed or were killed. Once more the arid land drank the heroes' blood.

Never had Agamemnon fought so gallantly, never had he struck and killed so many enemies. It seemed that nobody could fight him and already some of the Trojans were retreating under his repeated assaults, when Coön (son of Antenor) suddenly confronted him and speared his arm. Howling with rage and pain Agamemnon turned round and killed his assailant, but was no longer able to hold up his shield against the hail of arrows. He could do nothing but drag himself to his chariot and withdraw.

'Agamemnon is fleeing!' Hector shouted. 'Attack now!' It was now the Greeks turn to fall back. Many in fact dropped their weapons in order to run faster. Diomedes who had fought alongside Odysseus, cursed and shouted, 'What in heavens are you doing, fleeing like sheep? Have you lost your strength all at once? Stay with me Odysseus, let us resist!'

In answering him, Odysseus exclaimed, 'I shall not run Diomedes, I shall stay by you and fight. But I am convinced that Zeus has again come to the Trojans' rescue and that there is very little hope left for us.'

However, both warriors turned their menacing faces towards the enemy and stood their ground. Hector rushed up to attack them but was grazed by a spear and forced to retreat. Mocking him Diomedes shouted 'Ha, you run Hector! But wherever you are I shall find you and I will make you fight to the end!'

Agamemnon is hurt in the arm by a spear

From the stern of the ship Achilles watches the various stages of the battle

He had barely ended his sentence when Paris shot an arrow which sank deep into Diomedes' right foot. Pain-stricken Diomedes stopped, cursing. The triumphant Paris gloated over him, 'You have been hit. I only wish I had been accurate and hit you in the stomach!'

'Damned fool!' replied Diomedes. 'I should like to see you without your bow, sword to sword! You wouldn't talk like this then!'

But already the Trojans were closing in on him, and he could not move, neither to defend himself nor to run. This time he would have been lost without Odysseus' intervention, who shielded him and carried on fighting single-handed against a hundred Trojans. He killed many but in the fierce fighting was unable to avoid a spear, thrown at him by Socus, son of Hippasus. The tremendous blow would have been fatal if Athene had not softened it.

Odysseus knew that he could not hold on much longer. Soon he would be forced to yield and it would mean death for him and for Diomedes. He then started shouting for help and through the din of the battle his cries reached Menelaus' ears who exclaimed, 'Odysseus needs help! Aias come with me, quick! Away we go!'

The battle rages on and turns in favour of the Trojans

Both dashed forward and found Odysseus covered in blood defending himself against a horde of enemies. Aias stepped in front of him using his gigantic shield to give them shelter. Behind this shelter, Menelaus was able to take Odysseus and Diomedes back to safety. Drained of all strength Menelaus had to help them on to the chariot before he could drive them back to the camp.

And so the Trojan onslaught continued, led by Hector and Paris. Paris, in keeping with his promise to the beautiful Helen, was trying to cancel the unimpressive proof of courage he had shown in battle until now. One after another, he sent vicious arrows from his bow inflicting death or painful wounds. One of them struck Machaon, the physician, which was a severe blow to the Greeks.

'Nestor!' shouted Idomeneus to the old warrior who was always present on the frontline, 'Machaon is worth a hundred men! Help him on to your chariot and take him to a shelter! We'll cover you!' As this was carried out the battle continued to rage, turning in favour of the Trojans who, step by step, moved toward the wall which protected the Greek tents and ships.

High above, at the stern of his ship resting on dry land, Achilles watched. Unperturbed, he had followed the various stages of the battle but now called to his loyal friend Patroclus and said, 'Patroclus, Nestor is driving a wounded man out of the battlefield. I cannot make out who it is but it looks like Machaon. Go and find out. Machaon is dear to me, he is a friend that I should never wish to lose.'

Patroclus set off running and found Nestor in his tent applying first aid treatment to Machaon who was in a bad state.

'Why is Achilles so concerned about Machaon?' exclaimed the old man. 'Many other Greeks have been wounded! Diomedes has been wounded, and so has Odysseus, and Agamemnon! ... We have reached our limit and what does he do? He watches us die!'

'He has been too deeply offended,' replied Patroclus, 'he won't fight.'

Nestor shook his white head and mumbled, 'This will be the end of us all. You Patroclus show that you are truly his friend and ask him to come to our rescue! And if he won't, then ask him to give you his weapons and come in his place! The Trojans will mistake you for Achilles, and daunted, they might relent!'

Patroclus dared not answer and ran back to Achilles' tent. Along the way he saw nothing but wounded men, worn out and resigned to defeat.

BOOK XII

So the Trojans pursued the Greeks who at first retreated beyond the trench and then clambered over their camp wall. From the top of it a hail of arrows rained on the attackers. In the dust and tumult the Trojans' chariots came to a halt, lining up along the edge of the trench which was strewn with bodies. Some charioteers pushed forward and tried to overcome the obstacle but the horses reared and neighed in fright at the sight of the ditch. It was impossible to drive them over.

'Hector!' shouted Polydamas, one of the bravest Trojans. 'It is senseless trying to cross the ditch with our chariots, let us leave them and cross on foot. If the Greeks attack us while we are in the chariots we are done for!'

'Yes!' Hector agreed, 'On foot! Forward!' and he leapt from his chariot. Never before had

The fight intensifies under the wall without allowing one moment's rest

victory seemed so close at hand. The ships were near and so were the supplies and arms storehouse. To loot and sack them would be to strike a fatal blow at the Greeks. Leading his men Hector crossed the trench on foot and reached the wall. There was a ceaseless and deadly exchange of arrows, stones and spears.

Protecting themselves with their shields, the Trojans moved forward to a reinforced gate which was being defended by the desperate Greek soldiers who knew full well that if they yielded all would be lost for them. Even those men, who, exhausted by the long struggle had needed to get their breath back, rest awhile and tend to their wounds, fought on relentlessly. There was no time left, this was a struggle for life and it did not tolerate one moment's rest.

Suddenly someone screamed 'The sky! Look at the sky!' They all looked up. Flying in the sky directly above the battlefield was a great eagle holding in its talons an enormous snake. The

snake, far from being dead, was writhing and hissing and trying to break free or pay dearly for its life. With a desperate contortion it lifted its head and sank its sharp fangs into the eagle's breast. Viciously bitten the great bird let out a shrill cry of pain, withdrew its talons and dropped its prey. The snake fell to the ground and slithered away. Polydamas, though brave that he was, turned pale.

'The snake is a sign from Zeus, Hector,' he said. 'I see it as an ill omen. I think Zeus is telling us that we will reach the ships but that the Greeks will harm us – seriously.'

'What are you saying, Polydamas?' exclaimed Hector. 'Do you think I care about eagles and snakes? I believe in battle only, and we are winning it! Are you afraid to fight, are you afraid to die? Beware, if you are thinking of retiring I shall be the one to kill you! Forward! Attack the gate! Trojans, let us knock it down!'

The commanding Hector led his men into attack, looking for a suitable place to make an opening through the wall. As it shook under the rocks thrown by the Trojans, so trembled the Greeks' hearts who continued defending themselves with lances, stones and arrows.

In the sky appears a great eagle holding an enormous snake trying to free itself

Hector seizes a large rock and hurls it against the gate

'Lycians, my valorous men, here! Stand by my side! With me! I cannot breach the wall on my own! Where is your courage? Why aren't you behind me? Forward! If we all unite, no one can resist us!'

Against the Lycians' massive onslaught Teucer's arrows and Aias' deadly spear had no effect. Both had to withdraw and, following Sarpedon, the Lycians at last hoisted themselves up on the wall with shouts of triumph. The battle became fiercer. Reinforcement battalions were sent in from both sides to join the battle. There was not a Greek or Trojan prince who was not spattered with blood, either his own or that of his enemy's, and yet there was no way of telling on which side victory was leaning. Suddenly out of the clangour and over the din of the battle, Hector's thundering voice rose 'Horse-tamer Trojans! Down with the wall, let us reach the ships and set them alight!'

All united in a supreme effort. Driven by an incredible strength, Hector seized a massive pointed boulder – so heavy that it would have been difficult for two men to lift – and hurled it against the gate, hitting the two iron bars which held its panels together. The colossal hinges shook, the iron bars gave way and the two panels shattered into splinters. A roar of triumph rose from the Trojans who at last saw the opening through which they would invade the enemy camp. The first one to leap forward was naturally Hector who held two spears in his hands. No one dared to confront him and anyhow no one would hold him now.

'Follow me! Follow me!' he shouted, turning to the men behind him, and already more gates were giving way. Here and there the wall was dotted with Trojans who had climbed over it, breaking the enemy's resistance and swarming the ramparts. Through the shattered gates, through the breaches, the Trojans poured into the Greek camp like a mighty river that had burst its banks and was flooding the plain.

There was nothing left for the Greeks to do but to retreat to the ships. More than a retreat, it was flight! The Greeks were unable to organize a line of defence and they were unable to halt and re-group. It seemed then that nothing could save the ships, and consequently the whole Greek army, from destruction and catastrophe.

Then forward stepped Sarpedon, leader of the Lycian warriors who had given their support to the Trojans. Protected by a large shield, Glaucus, another Lycian prince, walked by his side. Behind them followed close ranks of warriors. Telemonian Aias and his brother Teucer rushed to oppose them. From the ramparts, which the Lycians had begun to scale, Teucer repelled Glaucus with an arrow, but Sarpedon stood firm. Zeus himself protected him. When Aias launched his spear with his usual outstanding power, it embedded itself full into the Lycian prince's shield, but didn't pierce through. Sarpedon, however, staggered under the blow, his arm numbed. This weakness lasted but a second and inspired by Zeus he recovered.

BOOK XIII

But something happened up in the heavens. Zeus, who had been watching the Trojan offensive, at last turned his gaze away from the battlefield. He was satisfied that in obeying his orders, none of the gods had interfered in the battles. There was no doubt then that Hector and his men would get to the ships. There was no need for him to remain any longer. The gods' father therefore boarded his resplendent carriage and drove off to visit the land of the horse-breeding Thracians.

He had barely gone, when Poseidon hastened to the battlefield, waving his trident. He was determined to bring help to the Greeks whom he favoured. He could not accept their destruction, he could not bear to watch them so, retreating and falling.

As Zeus leaves on his chariot, Poseidon hastens to the Greeks' rescue

*Peisander and Menelaus confront each other in a
fierce duel*

Amongst the scampering Greek troops, he assumed the appearance of Calchas and accosted Telamonian Aias and Aias of Oïleus and shouted to both, 'There is in you enough power to save the whole army! What is the matter with you? Why do you think in terms of defeat and not of victory? Do not stay here. To battle, go back to battle!'

And with these words he tapped the two warriors with his magic staff lending them ardour and heroic spirit. The Trojans who pressed their advance further towards the ships suddenly met a counter attack. Until then the Trojan army had behaved like a boulder hurtling down a mountain, leaping wildly from rock to rock, mowing down everything on its path. But now, once it had reached the plain it was like it had lost its momentum and had slowly come to a

halt. So the Trojans halted before the Greeks, who influenced by the two Aias' were displaying renewed resistance.

In the bloody encounters that followed, many heroes fell on both sides, and over their bodies the struggle continued furiously. They fought in various places, under the ships' sterns. They fought with spears and swords, chariots clashed, the ground was cluttered with the dead and the moaning wounded. The earth was drenched with blood, littered with shattered spears, broken arrows, shields, helmets which had been torn off warriors' heads, lances that had not reached their target. Duels were fought between heroes, entire divisions of roaring soldiers came to grips with each other and in the chaos and heat of the combats, it was difficult to distinguish one's enemy from one's friend.

It was a glorious day for Idomeneus, King of the Cretans, who fought alongside the Greeks. But it was also a great day for Deiphobus, Priam's son and also for Aeneas, and for Paris and for the other Trojans. Supported by Poseidon, the Greeks were fighting bravely, and now that Zeus was looking elsewhere and was no longer keeping an eye on the battle, the Trojans suffered painful losses. In the battle Menelaus was tackled by young Peisander. Their vibrating spears drew no result, so they grasped their swords and engaged in a fierce exchange of blows and Peisander was killed.

Everywhere the wavering Trojan lines were driven back. Harpalion, prince of the Paphlagonians, allies of Troy, was struck dead by an arrow. He was immediately avenged by Paris who shot Euchenor, King of Corinth, with his unerring bow. On the whole, the left wing of the Trojan army was retreating.

Polydamas then ran in search of Hector who was fighting on the right wing. 'Hector,' he called out, 'we must call our troops or we will have fought in vain. There is no strategy in our attack!'

'You are right,' replied Hector, leaping from his chariot, 'stay here while I go to the left wing and give them orders!'

Hector's presence and voice restored new life to the Trojans. They reassembled to face the enemy frontline who stopped in their tracks. Hector dashed incessantly up and down the front ranks. Aias, upon seeing him, made his way through the soldiers and defied him.

'Hector!' he roared. 'Where do you think you are going? To our ships? You are mistaken. You will not get through! Only one path is open to you, that is the path of flight!'

'No Aias,' replied Hector, 'I shall not flee. Instead, this day shall be the Greeks' last! And yours too if you stand in my way! Before nightfall the dogs and the birds will feast over your body!'

The two of them attempted in vain to confront each other but the swaying ranks pulled them apart. Hector again shouted, 'Forward, Trojans! Stand by me! To the ships!'

His cry was echoed by a deafening roar emitted by a thousand men. Once more the Trojans attack met with a brave resistance put up by the Greeks who answered with their own cry of war.

Hector urges the Trojans to aim for the Greek ships

However slow, however difficult the Trojans' progress was towards the ships, Hector's cries reached the tent where old Nestor, sitting by the wounded Machaon, awaited news of the battle's latest developments.

'Unfortunately,' he whispered, 'Hector's cries are all too clear. I shall not remain in this tent. I shall take up my post!'

The old man felt that his time had come. He armed himself from head to toe and set off to combat but he was to die in battle, crowning his long life with glory. On his way he met some of the Greek princes who had gathered on the seashore. They were all worn out or wounded.

'Ah, Nestor!' Agamemnon said. 'Hector's threats have proved true! We are defeated and our ships shall be destroyed!'

'Yes,' replied the old man, 'the wall on which we had rested all our hopes has fallen, and it will not be up to us – I so old and you so wounded – to reverse the fortunes of the battle.'

'However,' suggested Agamemnon, 'we can launch the ships to sea and so avoid them from being destroyed by the Trojans. We could sail offshore, wait for nightfall and ...'

Odysseus interrupted him, 'Agamemnon, what cowardly words you speak! You who have the honour of leading the Greeks, you speak of taking flight? After nine years of battle and sacrifices you suggest putting our ships back to sea? Don't you understand that if they see a sailing ship, none of our warriors will want to get on it? They will think they have been betrayed. They will throw down their arms. It would be disastrous!'

'I agree, Odysseus!' replied Agamemnon. 'Speak then. What do you suggest we do?'

Diomedes intervened 'Listen to me,' he said forcefully, 'we are really wasting too much time, we are wounded, it is true, and we cannot fight. Nevertheless we can stand among the fighters and urge them with our presence and voice. We can lead back to battle our scattered soldiers. Let us not linger therefore! Let's go where there is fighting!'

Fearing a Greek defeat, Nestor decides to go and fight

Thereupon the princes returned to what could have been the last battle had not Hera, protectress of the Greeks, kept a close watch over them. She did not want the triumph of Troy through the deaths of Agamemnon, Nestor, Odysseus and Diomedes.

'Zeus could be back any moment now,' she thought, 'to take the battle in hand, and there would then be no hope left. I must therefore distract his attention. I must act so that he doesn't see or think ...'

The beautiful goddess then flew over the high peaks of Mount Ida where Zeus had taken his seat again. Before she joined the father of all gods, she called on Sleep, brother of Death. 'Sleep,' she said, 'friend and master of all, listen to me. I have a favour to ask of you. Grant me my wish and you will receive a golden chair as a gift. Make Zeus, whom I am about to visit, sink into a deep sleep.'

'I cannot unless he asks me himself. I fear his anger.'

'Sleep, if you think a golden throne is not sufficient, I promise you shall marry one of the young Graces, the sweet Pasitheë with whom you are in love.' At these words Sleep smiled. 'If you give me Pasitheë whom I love, then, O Hera, I shall make Zeus sleep for as long as you wish!'

And so it happened. Followed by the invisible Sleep, Hera pleasantly conversed with Zeus, cajoling and caressing him, while Sleep cast his spell. Slowly Zeus fell asleep. As soon as Sleep saw the father of gods asleep, he fled to Poseidon. 'Now' he announced, 'you are free to help the Greeks, O Poseidon, king of the sea!'

Granting Hera's request, Sleep lulls Zeus into a deep sleep

Aias picks a large rock and flings it on Hector who falls unconscious

Poseidon did not hesitate. 'Warriors of Greece!' he shouted as he appeared to them, 'Are we to leave victory to Hector? No! Take courage! Let us unite our efforts and form an iron wall that the Trojans will not be able to overcome! Forward!'

Revived, the Greeks tightened their ranks and marched on slowly towards the Trojans, uttering loud shouts and raising a din of weapons. Neither the wind blowing through the leaves of the great oaks, not the roaring fires in the mountain ravines, nor the sea crashing on the reef were as loud as the clamour raised by the two opposing armies.

Hector saw all the enemy princes draw nearer – even the wounded ones – but he didn't lose heart at the sight. He wielded his spear and aimed it at Aias. The blow would have killed Aias had it not hit the heavy leather belt which held his shield and sword. As Hector, still facing the enemy, withdrew amongst his men, Aias picked up one of the many boulders that had been used to prop the ships and hurled it at him. The boulder stuck Hector on the head and he collapsed unconscious to the ground.

With a cry of triumph, the Greeks lunged forward hoping to capture their hated enemy. But already the Trojan warriors were shielding Hector. They had all rushed to his rescue: Aeneas, Polydamas, Agenor, Glaucus, Sarpedon, all the Trojan princes. While a close-linked rank held firm against the Greeks' lunge, Hector was dragged back, carried into a chariot and driven to the shore of the River Xanthus. There he was revived by cold water being poured over his head. He came to, opened his eyes, looked around him, then suddenly vomited blood and lost consciousness again.

Meanwhile, the Greeks were attacking with renewed zeal. This was the opportunity they had been waiting for, the moment which might decide the fate of the day. Before Hector recovered they must hurry and strike the enemy a hard blow.

For a while, even without Hector, the Trojans held on, but many perished, others fell back, the front line yielded and soon the retreat turned to flight. Chased by the Greeks, the Trojans lost all the ground they had conquered at such a high price. They were driven further and further back until they were compelled to clamber over to the other side of the wall!

The infuriated Zeus turns to Hera who has tricked him

BOOK XV

By now, the Trojans were on the brink of defeat, but suddenly Zeus awoke from his deep sleep. From the heights of Mount Ida, he turned his gaze towards the plain of Troy and saw the attacking Greeks led by the enraged Poseidon. He saw Hector lying unconscious on the bank of the River Xanthus and immediately understood. He turned to Hera who sat by him waiting anxiously, and glared at her with flashing eyes.

'Ah! So this is what you were up to!' he thundered. 'You have tricked me, you had me put to sleep! Beware Hera,' he went on, swollen with divine fury, 'you know what my wrath is like! Remember when I hung you by your feet and left you dangling from the clouds! I can do it again!'

Pale and tembling Hera answered, 'I never prompted Poseidon to go against the Trojans, believe me, Zeus. If you wish me to, I shall run down to him at once and tell him to leave the field...'

'No! I shall not send you,' replied Zeus, 'instead you will fetch Iris and Apollo – they will carry out my orders. I have promised Thetis,' he went on more calmly, 'to do justice to her son Achilles whom Agamemnon has offended. And I shall. The Greeks shall be brought to the brink of defeat and then realize that without Achilles' help they can achieve nothing. When they reach this conclusion, Achilles will take up his arms again ... Ah, then I shall let Troy fall and Hector die. Until then,' he concluded, 'let no one dare

49

Iris goes to Poseidon and orders him to withdraw

stay there!' Poseidon was livid with anger and humiliation, but he could not disobey. Reluctant and cursing he went back to the sea and was immersed by the waves. Meanwhile, Zeus addressed Apollo, 'Go down to the banks of the River Xanthus. There you will find Hector unconscious. Give him back his strength and stay by his side. Help him in battle!'

Apollo swept down from Mount Ida and in a flash appeared before Hector. He had not yet recovered, he was still stunned and out of breath, but had managed to sit up on a stone.

'What are you doing here Hector?' asked the god. 'You have been hit I know. For a while you feared lest you should die, I know that too. But you won't. I am Apollo and I have been sent by Zeus to tell you to take your post and start after the Greeks again. Stand up! Go and fight! Remember I shall be by your side!'

The Trojans counter-attack the Greeks taking them by surprise

intervene to help the Greeks! And now Hera, off with you!'

As quick as lightning Hera flew to Olympus where the gods, seeing her arrive pale and distraught, gathered round her.

'Zeus is much angered,' she told them, 'let none of us dare stand in his way! Oh, it is terrible, terrible! Iris,' she added turning to the young divine messenger, you must run to Poseidon at once and tell him that Zeus commands him to leave the battlefield immediately and not to return there again. Apollo go at once to Zeus who wants to send you on a mission! Quickly do as I say! I am telling you, Zeus is beside himself with anger.'

Soon after, Iris flew to Poseidon who, trident in hand, was still inciting the Greeks to battle.

'Poseidon,' she said, 'I bring you an order from Zeus. Leave here, return to your sea and

Upon hearing these words, Hector felt all his strength returning to him. He felt his muscles flex and his blood rush through his veins. He stood up, grasped his spear, he picked up his shield, mounted his chariot and joined the bewildered troops.

'Follow me!' he bellowed. 'Back to the assault brave Trojans! We must reach the wretched ships and set them on fire! Follow me!' As one, the Trojans followed, facing the enemy again. And again the fortunes of the long battle turned. The Greeks who thought they had already won, saw Hector fall upon them. Aghast and frightened, they faltered, dismantled the ranks and fled. The first one to recover his courage was Thoas who shouted, 'Hector is not dead, Zeus is on his side, but let us gather princes of Greece! Let us cover our army's retreat so as to enable them to form new ranks in defence of the ships!'

At this call, the strongest fighters rushed to form a barrier which held back the Trojans for a while. Behind them, in the meantime, the main body of the forces fled in a panic towards the sea! Against Thoas and his men, several Trojan assaults failed, but it was the Greeks who were dying in ever increasing numbers.

'Never mind the dead!' Hector shouted to his companions who stopped to strip the corpses. 'Leave their armours and shields! We shall have time to collect them after the victory. Everyone to the ships now, and take the blazing torches with you. Victory is ours!'

Like a river bursting its banks and flooding the plain uncontrollably, so the Trojans moved seaward, gathering in close formation around the ships where the Greeks had retreated in a last effort to defend them. Heedless of the arrows and spears raining on him, Hector tried to set fire to the first ship. From the high stern, however, the Greeks protected the ship with the strength of desperation.

'Now is the time to die or save ourselves!' shouted Aias, trying to infuse courage into his men. To which Hector replied 'Bring the fire! Zeus is with us. When we have destroyed these ships, Troy will be saved!'

Heedless of the spears and arrows, Hector tries to set fire to a Greek ship

BOOK XVI

While the fighting continued Patroclus burst into his lord Achilles' tent. Turmoil, shouts, screams and moans could be heard close by. Yet here in the Myrmidon camp there was perfect order and a strange, eerie silence. In his tent, Achilles dressed in a simple tunic, sat quietly, as though the war he had so bravely fought in for nine years no longer concerned him. But seeing Patroclus so distraught, pale and drenched in perspiration, Achilles' face became sombre.

'What is the matter with you Patroclus?' he asked. 'You look as though you've been crying. You are crying! Why? Do you bring news of a friend's death? Or do you weep,' he added, 'because the Trojans are setting fire to the ships?'

'Yes, noble Achilles, my Lord! That is the cause! Too many are dead and wounded! If you returned to battle ...'

'No,' interrupted Achilles. 'No, Patroclus. I have been too deeply offended to fight again for Agamemnon.'

'Then,' implored the youth, 'at least allow me to fight, lend me your armour, your helmet and let me lead the Myrmidons into the field. The Trojans will think I am Achilles coming to assist the Greeks, and perhaps will not dare press their attack!'

Achilles hesitated then said, 'So be it! If that is your wish Patroclus, take my soldiers and fight. Yes,' he added, 'by saving our ships we are saving our way home. Yes, bring me glory so that Agamemnon will realize his error and will give me back Briseis. But,' he went on, looking sternly at his young friend, 'hear my advice. As soon as you have repelled the Trojans from the ships, return to our quarters. Beware of letting yourself being carried away by your longing for victory, do not follow the enemy! You must not,' he insisted, 'take from me, the honour of entering the city of Troy. And more importantly, I don't want you to take risks. Drive back the enemy, Patroclus and then let the Trojans fight on their own. Get ready now,' he concluded rising to his feet, 'I shall assemble my men.'

Patroclus could not suppress a cry of joy and he began to put on the splendid armour, which even on its own was sufficient to deter any enemy. Meanwhile Achilles prepared his Myrmidons for battle.

'I shall not be the one to lead you to the enemy,' he shouted, 'but by following Patroclus, you shall be following me! Let each of you fight with all his might!'

The eager men leapt off Achilles' fifty ships. At that moment Patroclus came out of the tent wearing the dazzling armour and cheers of enthusiasm welcomed him. He jumped into his battle chariot driven by the charioteer Antomedon and to which were harnassed the formidable horses – Balius and Xanthus. And off he set to battle.

Achilles watched him leave, and then returning to his tent he took out from a richly inlaid chest, a cup, from which no other man but he had ever drunk. After cleaning it, he filled it up with wine.

'I drink to you, Almighty Zeus!' he said solemnly. 'I am sending my friend Patroclus to battle. Give him strength, let everyone see that he can fight on his own, let him drive back the Trojans from the ships and let him return safe and sound to my camp.'

With these words, he slowly drank and emptied the cup. And Zeus heard his prayer. Of these two wishes he granted the first, but not the second. Patroclus was indeed to repel the Trojans but he was not to return to Achilles' tent.

Patroclus' and the Myrmidons' arrival infused courage into the Greeks and at the same time appalled the Trojans who thought they were facing the invincible Achilles. They drew back, then abandoned a ship to which they had finally set fire. Fighting continued amongst the ships but under the pressure from Patroclus and his warriors, there was nothing Hector could do but to call back his troops and flee.

Many were the Trojans who challenged Patroclus for they had realized that he was not

Achilles. One by one, the young warrior struck them down. Even the stalwart Sarpedon, King of the Lycians, fell, his heart pierced by a spear. It seemed that Patroclus was just as strong as Achilles and that nobody could stand in his way. Then Hector drove straight at him in his chariot, steered by Cebriones the charioteer. Patroclus waited, a spear in one hand, a stone in the other. At the opportune moment he threw the stone with all his strength which hit Cebriones full on the forehead. He rolled in the dust, while the chariot, no longer steered, veered dangerously. In readiness, Hector had jumped off the chariot

just in time to push back Patroclus who had pounced on the charioteer's body.

The fierce duel between the two warriors soon became a ferocious battle. Around Cebriones' corpse fell a hail of arrows and the Trojans and the Greeks fought fiercely. Swept by the ardour of the battle, Patroclus forgot Achilles' advice to retire directly after the enemy had been driven back from the ships. The ships were by now far behind and Troy was getting closer and closer. There Patroclus ventured, slaying furiously at everything in his way. There he was destined to find death.

Patroclus flings a stone at Hector's charioteer

BOOK XVII

During the violent fight over Cebriones' body, Achilles' young friend was in fact stabbed in the back by a spear thrown by Euphorbus. His armour came undone and his helmet – Achilles' pride – rolled in the dust. The wound was not mortal but Patroclus felt that he could no longer fight. Staggering and losing blood he dragged himself back amongst the Myrmidons. But Hector saw him and did not hesitate. He lunged at him with a spear and stabbed him below the belt. Without uttering a sound Patroclus fell to the ground.

'You thought you would take Troy, Patroclus!' Hector exclaimed triumphant. 'Instead I have killed you! This is the end of the road for you! You will not enter my city but you shall serve as a meal to the vultures!'

'That's right, Hector,' replied Patroclus with a failing voice, 'boast about my death. You have not long to live. Achilles himself will avenge me. You shall perish by his hand ...'

'Who knows?' retorted Hector, 'Perhaps Achilles is to die before me?' But Patroclus could no longer hear him; he was dead. Hector then stripped him of his armour and put it on himself, and on his head he placed the helmet that belonged to Achilles, his greatest rival.

Watching Hector's vainglorious act, Zeus muttered, 'Ah, unfortunate warrior! You wear the arms of someone who is feared by all and you cannot feel that death is close upon you! No, your wife Andromache will not see Achilles' armour and helmet. I shall not allow you to bring them back to her as trophies. But in exchange for death which is soon coming to you Hector, I want to give you a great victory today!'

Hector puts on Achilles' armour after stripping it off Patroclus

Greeks and Trojans fight over Patroclus' body in a ferocious battle

And once again Hector felt driven forward. Wielding his spear he renewed his assaults on the enemy. They fought furiously over Patroclus' body. The Greeks would not tolerate to see it taken to Troy and thrown to the dogs. The Trojans, on their part, could not lose such a testimony of their triumph.

Taking the first stand in defending the blood-drenched body was Menelaus, who stabbed the young Euphorbus to death. Then Menelaus was joined by the awesome giant Telamonian Aias. Together they held back the first Trojan on-slaught on their own. Gradually more warriors came to their rescue and Patroclus' body was fought over mercilessly. On the one hand, holding him by his head and arms, the Greeks tried to

pull him to safety towards the sea. On the other, tugging at his feet, the Trojans attempted to drag the corpse into Troy. Streams of blood gushed everywhere.

Amongst the swaying ranks of the medley whose intensity never abated, Hector and Aias looked for each other, never succeeding in coming face to face. It was almost impossible to tell whether it was day or night or even whether the sun or the moon shone above them. Over the battlefield hung a blanket of dust under which the opponents clashed, struck, fell, killed, wounded or died. It was to be a day of intolerable exhaustion, a day of stifling heat, a day without pause in which many would die.

'Greeks! We cannot return to our ships with-

out Patroclus' body!' someone shouted. 'We would rather the earth swallowed us alive!'

'Trojans!' came the answering cry. 'Even if you are all killed beside the corpse, let none of us retreat!'

Far from the conflict, Achilles' horses, Balius and Xanthus, had come to a halt and standing motionless they wept. Indeed, hot tears were streaming down their eyes, and dropped to the dusty ground. The animals mourned their Patroclus who had so often steered and driven them. Seeing their grief, Zeus himself was moved.

'No!' he said troubled, 'No, I promised you that Hector would never drive you! Take heart and do not be afraid to cross the battlefield in order to carry the loyal charioteer Automedon

back to the safety of the camp to rest.'

Escaping the reins of the ailing Automedon, the two neighing steeds galloped off and entered the battle at full speed making their way through the bewildered fighters. They pressed across the battlefield like a terrible vision and finally reached the seashore.

The day was drawing to its end and the fate of Patroclus' body was still uncertain.

'One of us,' shouted Menelaus 'must go to Achilles with the news of his friend's death. Perhaps when he finds out he will come himself to save his friend's body! Antilochus,' he went on, turning to a companion 'the sad duty falls to you. Go to Achilles and tell him that Patroclus is dead!'

BOOK XVIII

Meanwhile, in his tent, Achilles was overcome by a dark premonition. His heart told him something terrible had happened. He stepped out of his tent and stood motionless listening to the rumbling of the battle ... It was growing nearer, as at first it had grown further ... The Trojans were therefore advancing again.

'Perhaps this means that Patroclus has been wounded or is dead?' thought Achilles. 'But how could it be possible? Did I not tell him not to press on towards Troy?'

At that moment Antilochus appeared: 'Achilles, an unforeseen misfortune has befallen us. Patroclus is dead. Hector has killed him and stripped him of his armour and they are fighting over his body.'

On hearing the news, Achilles was thunderstruck. For a second darkness dropped over his eyes, for a second he was drained of his blood. Then he let out a howl of grief to the sky and fell to the ground in great convulsions as though he had lost his mind. He poured ash over his head, tore at his hair with his own hands under the eyes of his appalled friends and slaves. Then he rose and held Antilochus' hand, who was weeping uncontrollably. Achilles ran to the sea. From the depths of the sea his mother Thetis heard his cries. At once, gliding over the waves, she reached the shore and came to him, 'What is it, dear child,' she asked. 'Perhaps the Trojans have not retreated from the ships they wanted to set alight? Perhaps ...'

'They did withdraw, Mother. But Patroclus is dead,' replied Achilles. 'I have lost him, I have lost my weapons. I have sent to death the friend whom I loved better than myself and now I can do nothing for him. Help me, Mother, help me to go back to battle and may my destiny take its course.'

Sadly Thetis said, 'Yes my son. I shall be back at dawn to bring you new weapons. I shall ask Hephaestus to forge them for you. Wait for me. Then you can go back to battle and may your destiny take its course!' With these words, Thetis vanished.

Thetis appears to Achilles and promises the help he seeks

Achilles weeps over Patroclus' body and swears to avenge his death

In the meantime the Trojans had launched a new attack, determined this time to get hold of Patroclus' corpse at all cost.

Achilles had started to weep again, when in a dazzling light appeared Iris, the messenger goddess.

'Patroclus' body is about to be lost and you, Achilles, you weep and do nothing!'

The hero muttered, 'Hera has sent you Iris, and you reproach me. But how can I go to battle when I have no weapons?'

'You need no weapons. Come out of your tent and show yourself at the trench where the Greeks are being driven back by Hector. Let them hear your voice. That will be enough. This is what Hera has to tell you.'

So Achilles left his tent. An aura of fire seemed to shine around his head. With long strides he moved toward the trench beyond which the battle raged. Taking a firm stand he let out a howl of grief, rage and threat ... The Trojans heard him and, perplexed, they came to a halt. Achilles cried again. The Trojans dared not press on, their princes held the horses back, looking round anxiously. Is Achilles returning to combat? No. But for the third time Achilles howled and suddenly the Trojans were panic-striken. They fled and never stopped running until they had taken refuge inside the city! So ended the day which could have brought them a decisive victory. The Greeks therefore retrieved Patroclus' body and carried it to Achilles' tent. Embracing it, Achilles wept.

'Patroclus,' he said, 'I promised to bring you home alive and covered in glory. I did not keep this promise, but I shall keep another one: before I join you in the kingdom of the dead, I shall kill Hector!'

Throughout the night wailing and lamentations rose from the distraught Greek camp.

Hephaestus forges new armour for Achilles

Meanwhile, Thetis had gone to Hephaestus, the blacksmith god, and had found him among his puffing bellows, hard at work, beating the anvil with his mighty hammer. As he saw her, Hephaestus rejoiced and limped over to Thetis. He had never forgotten how she had hidden him and given him shelter in the sea when, as a child, he had run away from home, where his mother – ashamed to have a crippled son – would have him locked up. 'Ask me whatever you wish, Thetis,' he said joyfully. If I can do it, I shall. Perhaps it is already done.'

Thetis told him about Achilles' sad story and concluded, 'So Hephaestus I have come to ask you to forge a helmet, a shield, leggings and armour for my son. He no longer has any of those for Hector, the murderer, has stripped them from his beloved Patroclus.'

'You shall have what you ask for,' replied Hephaestus and at once he set to work in his smoke-filled workshop. First he made the shield: huge, sturdy with a triple rim, and he engraved it with the symbols of the earth, the sea and constellations of the heavens, also with pictures of cities, temples and rural labour scenes. Then he started on the armour and forged one brighter than the blazing fire. He shaped a tall shining helmet to fit perfectly on Achilles' head. And on top of it he placed a golden crest trailing a long horse's tail. As for the leggings, he used tin so that they would be light to wear and would not hinder his running. Never had a mortal seen more beautiful or stronger weapons. When Hephaestus had at last finished, he handed the arms to Thetis who swept down like a falcon from Mount Olympus, to take them to her son.

60

BOOK XIX

Achilles was still weeping over Patroclus' body when Thetis arrived with her shimmering load. 'My son,' she said 'stop crying! Here are the weapons you have asked for. Hephaestus has forged them for you. Put them on and let your destiny take its course.'

At the sight of the weapons, the Myrmidons around Achilles whispered in utter wonder, so great was the impression of might given by the armour, helmet and shield. Achilles carefully surveyed the gifts from his mother and Hephaestus, and said, 'Before I wear these to battle, it is necessary that I reconcile myself with Agamemnon. I am already paying too bitterly for the anger caused by the offence. I pray you divine mother, save Patroclus' body from decay!'

'I will, my child. But do not linger, do your duty.'

Achilles went to the seafront and with a thunderous voice called for the Greek troops to assemble. Hearing his voice and his words, the Greeks trembled with anticipation and hurried on to the centre of the camp. There in front of all the princes, many of whom were wounded, Achilles walked towards Agamemnon with outstretched arms in a sign of peace and solemnly declared that he renounced any thought of anger and revenge.

'I can see,' he said, 'that our feud has only proved beneficial to Hector. But let us now forget the past. Let bygones be bygones, Agamemnon. We must only think of fighting. Come lead your army to battle, I shall be at your side.'

Achilles walks to Agamemnon with outstretched arms in a sign of peace

Moved, Agamemnon replied, 'Greeks, friends, I should like to say that when I offended the noble Achilles, I was not myself. I know I was wrong but, believe me, it was not I who spoke, it was not I who offended. It was as though a demon had taken possession of me. No, Achilles, I am not responsible for the outrage I have caused you. What has been has been, you are right, but I want to make amends even for a wrong that was not of my doing. You shall receive from me all the gifts you want, and with them you shall receive my friendship!'

'The gifts can wait,' exclaimed Achilles, 'let us turn our thoughts to battle. Let us go now!'

Odysseus, who had been wounded during the fight, rose to speak, 'No Achilles, we cannot go to battle now. You come with us and victory shall not escape us. But, my friend, we are still too worn by the tough struggle we have just sustained. Only a few of us and our warriors have had a chance to eat, and you mighty Achilles, are well aware that strength depends on nourishment. Let us first take some food then we shall resume our fight with renewed energy.'

Achilles listened impatiently to these wise and prudent words. He wanted to avenge Patroclus at once. But everyone agreed with Odysseus. Before he prepared for battle, Agamemnon sent Achilles the most precious gifts: seven tripods, twelve mettlesome horses, twenty splendid copper vases, ten gold talents and seven young slaves all talented at domestic work. Then solemnly and according to Greek tradition they carried out the sacrifices for the consecration of peace and reconciliation. Finally, the young and beautiful Briseis, who had been the cause of the fatal anger, was taken back to Achilles' tent. When the young girl saw Patroclus' corpse she knelt by it and began to wail, scratching her cheeks and breasts in despair.

'Alas, my very dearest Patroclus,' she moaned, 'I shall never be able to speak to you again, we shall never again make plans for the future. I have found you but never as I thought I would: dead, you are dead!' They all wept and Achilles looked on somberly. And he remembered the time when they had spoken of war together.

'Patroclus, I shall die under the walls of Troy,' Achilles would often say, 'such is my destiny: a brief but glorious life. But you Patroclus, you will go back to Greece and you will relate my exploits . . .'

The beautiful Briseis is taken back to Achilles' tent

Odysseus and the other princes urged Achilles to take food. Weakness could overcome him in battle and betray him. But the youth stubbornly refused to eat or drink! From the peaks of Olympus, Zeus then turned to Athene, 'Just like a child, Achilles does not want to eat. Still he must not be left to starve. Run my daughter and distil into his breast some nectar and ambrosia – divine food – so that he will not be robbed of his strength in the middle of the battle.'

Athene promptly obeyed and suddenly Achilles felt his usual strength return to him. He stood up wiping away the last tears. It was no time to weep but to fight. The Greek warriors sitting between the ships and the wall so bitterly fought over earlier, had now eaten and prepared for battle. Achilles gave orders for the Myrmidons to be ready to move on, then he started to dress. With eyes blazing like fire and gnashing teeth he slipped on the armour forged by Hephaestus, fastened his sword belt, secured the shield on his arm and, finally, placed on his head the helmet adorned with the shimmering horse tail. He then entered his tent and took from a case a formidable spear, so long and heavy that he was the only one among the Greeks who was able to handle it.

When he reappeared he was greeted by roaring cheers from the whole army, Automedon then drew up in the battle chariot to which Xanthus and Balius were harnassed, both pawing the ground impatiently. Achilles leapt onto the carriage and with a deep voice said, 'Xanthus, Balius, when the fighting is done, bring me back alive! Don't leave me there dying on the field as you left Patroclus!'

Through a miracle performed by Hera, Xanthus answered, 'Yes Achilles, we shall save you. But remember the hour of your death is drawing near. And on that hour we can be of no help even if we run like the wind. It is your destiny, Achilles to be defeated in battle by a man and god!'

Stamping his foot impatiently the hero replied, 'Xanthus, why do you speak of death? I know that I must die here, far from home! But before this happens, I will have avenged Patroclus and defeated the Trojans. Let's go now!'

With that he gave the cry of war and ordered his charioteers to set off. So leading the Greeks forward, the city of Troy appeared in the distance, tightly enclosed within its walls.

Achilles puts on the new armour forged for him by Hephaestus

BOOK XX

The battle between Greeks and Trojans was about to start again. And up above on the peaks of Olympus Zeus called all the gods to a solemn assembly. He insisted that all be present. With great sternness he said, 'This is a decisive time in the war. I shall not move from here but you may intervene in the battle according to each of your likes and dislikes!'

At these words the gods immediately flew down to the plain which stretched between the city and the sea. Athene, Poseidon, Hephaestus and Hera sided with the Greeks. Aphrodite, Ares, Apollo and Artemis with the Trojans. As soon as the immortals touched down on the battlefield, the fight began furiously.

Flying into a temper amongst the clashing troops, Achilles on his chariot, searched for Hector in order to challenge him. Ares noticed it

and came up to Aeneas, 'Aeneas, Achilles is approaching. Go to him, stop him, kill him! You will reap eternal glory and you will save Troy!'

Aeneas knew he was not as strong as Achilles. He had already fought him once, yet he did not hesitate. He stepped forward and upon seeing him Achilles shouted, 'Why do you come to me, Aeneas? Do you think you can defeat me and so be rewarded by Priam with the crown of Troy? No, listen to me. Go back now, unless you want to die!'

'Your chatter will not make me run Achilles!' replied Aeneas, and he launched his spear which for all its speed and power was not able to pierce Achilles' shield – the work of a god. The young Greek, in his turn sent his spear whistling through the air and it pierced Aeneas' shield like a bolt of lightning. The bronze-headed spear

Achilles and Aeneas fight each other in a duel and Poseidon protects Aeneas

missed Aeneas by a hair's breath and sank into the ground beside him. Achilles unsheathed his sword, Aeneas picked up a rock and brandishing it over his head was just about to throw it. The duel would certainly have ended with the death of one or the other hero if Poseidon had not intervened.

'No,' he whispered, 'I do not want Aeneas to die. A great destiny is reserved for him – that of perpetrating the Trojan race through the centuries!' And he flew ahead and sprayed a dense mist around Achilles whose vision became blurred. Poseidon then pulled the spear from the ground, laid it at Achilles' feet and swept Aeneas off, propelling him to the very back of the Trojan ranks.

'Do not fight with Achilles again,' he warned, 'but know that when he is dead and gone, no other Greek shall ever defeat you!' Having spoken these words, Poseidon returned to where Achilles was and lifted the mist. The hero saw his spear lying at his feet, but no Aeneas.

'This is indeed a miracle,' he muttered. 'Anyhow, I knew that Aeneas is loved by the gods . . . Well, never mind,' he exclaimed, and picking up his spear he called to his men, 'there are other Trojans to kill! Friends, follow me, I cannot deal with them alone and fight for you all! Let each one of you confront his opponent and slay him as I shall do!'

For his part, Hector was encouraging the Trojans, who at the sight of Achilles were already faltering.

'You must not be afraid of this man!' he shouted, 'They have taken Troy with words but they never will in reality! Were he made of fire, I would still challenge Achilles!' His men answered him with a cry of war and the din of the battle.

Achilles was achieving wonders killing, one after another, numerous Trojan heroes. When the very young Polydorus, Hector's brother, fell, Hector was overcome with grief and sought instant revenge. Making his way among the fighters, he sought to challenge his rival in a duel. Achilles shouted, 'Come Hector! Come and meet your end!'

'Don't try to frighten me!' replied Hector and he cast his lance. He would not have missed had not Athene, as quick as lightning, warded it off, saving Achilles in the nick of time. Achilles then prepared to strike but it was Apollo's turn to intervene. He hid Hector in a dense cloud where Achilles threw his spear four times, in vain.

Hector throws his spear at Achilles but Athene diverts it and saves him

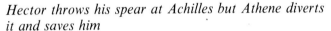

'Ah, so you escape me, you cur!' he exclaimed. 'A god has saved you again, but I'll have done with you. Do you hear me, Hector? Sooner or later I'll have done with you!'

He returned to his chariot and whipping the horses, Automedon the charioteer plunged into the thick of the battle. Like a fire blown by a gale destroying dry forests, so Achilles swept the enemy ranks, mowed down Trojans who stood in his way and trampled the wounded men, in his uncontrollable fury. The chariot's wheels, the axle and the hooves of Xanthus and Balius were spattered with blood, and also covered in blood advanced the invincible Achilles.

BOOK XXI

The Trojans withdrew in panic. The disorder turned into irreparable chaos when they reached the Scamander river. Terrified, they fell into the water, seeking salvation on the opposite bank, hoping that Achilles' chariot would not be able to cope with the current. But Achilles leapt from the chariot and taking only his sword, he chased after the fugitives across the water and slaughtered them. Nobody dared to stand up against him, nobody dared to turn round and face him. Finding no resistance, the hero killed without respite, without mercy, not even for those who, unarmed and wounded surrendered and begged to be spared! Soon the river became tinged with the dark colour of blood, soon horrendous islands of corpses surged to the surface. Helmets, shields, armours cluttered the banks and amongst the dead floated the spears. In the water the implacable Achilles continued to strike.

At the sight of so much blood and such ferocity, the god who lived in the depths of the Scamander river swelled its waters and crashed them against Achilles. The waves lashed and choked him, blinding him, overwhelming him in an attempt to knock him down and crush him against the sand and mud. Weighed down by his armour, Achilles struggled desperately and realized that he had reached the limits of his strength.

'Is it then to be so,' he moaned. 'Am I to drown like an imbecile?'

The god of the Scamander river swells its waters crashing them against Achilles

Ares and Athene quarrel and engage in an open battle

Indeed that would have been his end had not Hephaestus rushed to save him by assaulting the river with his flames and compelling it, after a hard struggle, to calm its waters and cease harassing the hero.

The fight between the Scamander river and the lame god triggered off a brief but heated feud between all of the gods. From the start of the Trojan war they had been divided. More than once they had disagreed and Zeus had had to threaten them so that they would not come to blows with each other, but now the time seemed to have come. Ares threw himself into the battle where Athene was already fighting furiously against the Trojans.

'Why are you here? Once you guided Diomedes' spear to wound me. Well now it is my turn!' And with this he struck a formidable blow on his sister's helmet. But the helmet could even withstand Zeus' thunderbolt and Ares' blow came to nothing. The goddess retorted at once by hurling a boulder which reached its target. Ares was hit in the neck. He groped blindly trying to keep his balance but his breath had been taken away and he stumbled onto his knees.

'You silly fool!' said Athene mockingly. 'You want to fight with me and you don't even know I am stronger than you!'

The lovely Aphrodite then rushed to Ares' help. She took him by the hand helped him to his feet and led him away from the field. The outraged Athene chased after her and knocked her down!

'Ha!' she exclaimed before her battered rivals, 'If we immortals had fought, the war would have been over long ago and Troy would no longer be standing!'

Meanwhile Poseidon had challenged Apollo but the latter had replied that he did not wish to fight. The haughty Artemis reproached him harshly, urging him to take up the challenge. But Hera flew to confront her.

She plucked the bow off Artemis' shoulder and beat her until she took refuge by Zeus' feet, in tears. It was to there, around their father, that all the gods finally returned when they had done with fighting. Some in triumph, some humbled, some vexed. But all the immortals maintained that the Greeks had shown more courage and determination.

Among the gods back at Olympus, Apollo was still missing. He had gone back to Troy, determined to defend it with his presence.

Inside the city old Priam climbed up the tower and watched the battle anxiously. When he saw his warriors withdraw in disorder, chased and slaughtered by Achilles, he ordered, 'Open the gates! Let our men find shelter in the city! But be careful to shut them in time, beware not to let Achilles in!'

His command was obeyed but how would the fleeing Trojans enter the city. They were by now trampling over each other, they would be crushed in the rush to cross the threshold. They would perhaps be slaughtered to the last! Apollo was well aware of it and so left Troy to try and avoid the catastrophe. He flew to Agenor, the valiant warrior, and inspired him with courage, calm and determination. Agenor who was running with the others, stopped at once.

'Why am I running?' he thought. 'Why do I let myself be driven by the others? I am not afraid of Achilles! He is a man like the rest of us and like the rest of us he can be killed. I shall not run but instead I shall face him!'

He turned around, wielding his spear, 'Achilles,' he shouted, 'do not think that you are going to sack Troy today. We are not all frightened of you!' And he launched his spear which struck Achilles under the knee, and had it not hit the leggng made by Hephaestus, it would certainly have broken Achilles' leg. In his turn, the unscathed Achilles prepared to attack. But Apollo intervened and surrounding Agenor with a mist, swept him off to safe ground. So that the Trojans could pass through the open gates, the god took on Agenor's appearance and appeared in front of the confused Achilles.

'So you are still here then!' the hero exclaimed, and brandishing his bloodstained spear, he threw himself in hot pursuit of the man he thought was Agenor and who was running desperately across the plain.

'I'll catch you up, coward!' shouted Achilles at his heels, and overcome as he was with rage and craze for revenge, he could not have imagined that the fugitive was not Agenor but Apollo in disguise. Neither did he realize that he was being led in the opposite direction of Troy. So the exhausted Trojans, no longer hounded by Achilles, were able to enter the city, close the gates and allow themselves at last, a little rest.

Achilles chases after Agenor on the plain not knowing that it is Apollo in disguise

*Hector sees Achilles advancing and waits for him,
spear in hand*

BOOK XXII

However, not all Trojans were able to enter the safety of the city. One of them remained outside the walls: Hector. There he stood alone in front of the Scaean gate, spear in hand, waiting.

Meanwhile Apollo had stopped running. He cast off Agenor's appearance and resumed his own. Then mockingly he turned to Achilles and said, 'Why are you chasing after me? Can't you see I am a god and that you cannot kill me because I am immortal?'

'A god indeed, the most disastrous of all!' replied Achilles angrily when he realized he had been made a fool of. 'If only I could kill you Apollo, I would take my revenge on you!' Then he spun round and dashed back towards Troy. From the tower, Priam saw him running back.

'Hector, my son,' he shouted, 'come inside the city! Take shelter, do not stand up to Achilles! Save yourself and with you save Troy!'

Hecuba, the hero's mother also begged and moaned and held out her arms in desperation. But Hector gave no answer. Yes, he had also seen Achilles approaching, he also felt that the supreme moment was close but he did not wish to go inside the city. He did not want to flee and mar his honour. He could have ordered his troops to retreat earlier, as soon as he had seen Achilles join the battle, but he had not done so and he would now pay for it. What was to be done? . . . Throw down his arms, surrender and return Helen back to the Greeks? . . . Hector knew full well that in any case Achilles would not grant him a moment's truce, that he would not accept his surrender, that he would not have mercy on him. Better to face him then, and at last one would know which one of them Olympus wanted to cover in glory!

A weighty silence fell on the entire plain and Hector and Achilles came face to face. Something quite unexpected then occurred. Hector, whose courage until then had been unswerving, was suddenly panic-stricken. Seeing his great rival advance on him, gigantic and menacing, surrounded by a magic aura of light as though the sun glowed through his bronze armour, Hector's heart faltered.

He was unable to look at the vision, he was unable to stand his ground. He turned his back on Achilles and fled. Yes, he fled, heedless of the Trojans who watched from the wall or the Greeks who had drawn closer in silence. He fled and circled the walls of Troy three times with Achilles at his heels.

Meanwhile, at Olympus, Zeus had been weighing Achilles and Hector's lives on his scales and saw that it was Hector's time to die.

'So be it!' he murmured solemnly.

That is when Athene played the last trick. Speeding down to Troy, she assumed the appearance of Deiphobus, Priam's son and caught up with Hector in full flight.

'Brother!' she cried. 'Stop! Don't wear yourself out so! Let us both confront Achilles, come!'

Out of breath Hector replied, 'Yes, Deiphobus, you are right. Enough of running! Achilles!' he shouted turning round, 'It is you and I now! Let us fight, but let the victor return the body of the defeated!'

Achilles draws his sword and runs towards Hector

Achilles answered, 'No I shall make no pact with you! You are as good as dead, Hector! You shall pay for what you have done to Patroclus!' He had barely finished his sentence, when Achilles launched his spear. Hector was ready for it and leapt aside and the lance sank into the ground.

'You have missed Achilles,' exclaimed Hector the Trojan, 'my turn now!' And he thrust his spear but it bounced off the shield made by Hephaestus.

Hector turned round, stretching his right arm: 'Deiphobus!' he cried, 'give me your spear . . .' He stopped short – there was no one about him. He understood and muttered, 'Ha! the gods are indeed calling me to death! This is one of Athene's tricks. Well I shall not die without glory!' He drew his sword and lunged at Achilles . . . but the latter had already raised his own spear which the invisible Athene had picked up and put back into his hand. Taken by surprise, Hector could do nothing to defend himself. He was struck in the neck by the deadly weapon and collapsed to the ground.

'You thought you would remain unpunished, Hector!' exclaimed Achilles, 'Now the dogs will have your body!'

'Achilles,' implored the dying Hector, 'by all that is sacred to you, I beseech you to return my body to Troy . . .' Then death took him.

While Troy resounded with cries of lament, the triumphant Greeks rushed forward, gathered round the fallen hero and savagely thrust their spears into his corpse!

'Ha!' they shouted, 'He is softer now than he was in battle!' Then Achilles tied Hector's feet to his chariot and howling, lashed his horses into a gallop. Dragging his rival's corpse in the dust, tearing it apart and defiling it, he drove round the walls of Troy before going back to his camp.

Achilles ties Hector's body to his chariot and drags it in the dust round the walls of Troy

BOOK XXIII

All the Greeks had by now rejoined their camp, removed their armour and put down their arms, at last thinking of resting. But Achilles ordered the Myrmidons to remain armed. 'Come with me!' he added. 'We must pay our respects to Patroclus, we shall rest afterwards!'

His orders were obeyed and together with his warriors, he wept on the seashore, calling out the name of his friend.

'I have kept my promise, Patroclus,' he sobbed. 'I have killed Hector and I have thrown his body to the dogs'.

The wailing rising from Troy was echoed by the weeping rising from the sea. Even after the Myrmidons had finally taken off helmet and armour, even after they had fallen to the ground in utter exhaustion, Achilles continued to lament, alone, on the vast beach.

The following day a huge pyre was prepared on which they put the embalmed body of Patroclus. Solemn sacrifices were carried out, then Achilles set fire to it.

'Be happy in the Kingdom of the Dead, Patroclus! You have been avenged!' In total silence, the Greeks watched the flames consume the young hero's body whose ashes were gathered and placed in a golden urn which was buried by the sea.

In the meantime, something strange had occurred. Not one dog had approached Hector's body which had been thrown in a corner. Apollo and Aphrodite had taken care of the poor mortal remains and protected it from further laceration.

Patroclus' funeral was over. But Achilles raised his hand and in the solemn silence he shouted, 'Friends, wait! Before you return to

The winner of the boxing match will be given an untamed mule and the runner-up a beautiful cup

trained in domestic work. The contenders were the gigantic Telamonian Aias and the shrewd Odysseus. The latter was shorter and not as strong as his opponent, but no less skilled. Grappling they both fought for a long time and neither one was able to bring the other down. The wrestling match dragged on and the spectators were getting bored.

'Let's do this,' said Aias, 'the first one to lift the other off the ground will be the winner. Agreed?'

'Agreed,' replied Odysseus. The first attempt was by Aias. He would easily lift his rival off the ground and he was about to do just that when Odysseus kicked him on the shin. Taken by surprise, Aias dropped to the ground. There was general bewilderment. Such a big man had yielded under Odysseus's weight? It was now Odysseus's turn, but as hard as he tried he could not lift his giant opponent. Achilles then intervened, 'You have both won and shall receive equal prizes!'

your tents, I ask you to honour one more time my beloved friend. In memory of him, I want you, valiant warriors, to measure your strength against one another. In the name of Patroclus I want you to compete in a contest of skill and power. I shall draw the prizes from the treasures of my war booty.'

And so a boxing match was suggested. The winner would be given an untamed mule and the runner-up a splendid cup. The noble Epeius stepped forward and challenged everyone by saying in a loud voice, 'Whoever wants to fight me can step out. But let your friends stand by to give you a hand when I'll have finished with you!'

Epeius was not boasting! After a brief fight, he knocked down, with a terrific punch, the only man who had accepted the challenge, Euryalus. He was carried unconscious and covered in blood to his tent. Achilles then suggested a wrestling match offering a huge tripod as first prize and for the loser a beautiful slave, well

The winner of the wrestling contest will receive a tripod and the runner-up a beautiful slave well skilled in domestic work

The games continued with a spear-throwing competition. At first the champions competed in a sort of duel: whoever succeeded in scratching his opponent's skin and draw a little blood would be the winner. The challenge was between Diomedes and Telamonian Aias. They confronted each other with great zeal but neither succeeded in wounding the other. The game then became dangerous. Indeed the contenders' fighting spirit was frightening and the concerned spectators called for the competition to be suspended and that both be given equal prizes.

More spear-throwing challenges followed. Agamemnon and Meriones presented themselves. Before the two of them could measure their skill, Achiles said, 'Agamemnon, every one knows that no one can surpass you in spear-throwing. Then take this copper vase and to you, Meriones, I give a sturdy lance!' All approved and with this gesture peace amongst the Greeks was sealed and the memory of the feud erased. Thus ended the games in honour of Patroclus.

An embossed silver dish will be awarded to the winner of the foot race. A fat ox will go to the runner-up and half a gold talent to the third contender

A foot race then took place for which the first prize would be an embossed silver dish. The runner-up would be given a well-fattened ox and the third contender half a gold talent. Moving forward there was Aias, son of Oïleus, followed by the young Antilochus, son of Nestor. And to everyone's surprise there came Odysseus, tired as he was from his struggle with Aias. From a line marked out by Achilles the three champions set off running. At once Aias took the lead distancing himself from Antilochus but he could not succeed in outrunning Odysseus who kept close behind. The spectators standing cheered as the two opponents covered the last stretch.

'Help me to win, Athene!' prayed Odysseus and the goddess came to his aid, making Aias trip and roll on the ground just as he was about to cross the finishing line. One stride and Odysseus won the race.

'You were helped by a goddess,' grumbled Aias. But Antilochus said, 'Well, I admit, young as I am, I can do nothing against old Odysseus!' And they all laughed heartily.

Diomedes and Telamonian Aias compete in a spear-throwing competion

75

Priam kneels before Achilles imploring him to return his son's body

BOOK XXIV

Several days went by without any fighting whatsoever. Achilles' grief did not abate. Every morning after spending the night wandering and sighing on the seashore, he tied Hector's corpse to his chariot and dragged it three times around Patroclus' tomb. The corpse of the dead hero did not decay, however, as Apollo had taken pity and protected it!

But he was not the only one to pity Hector. The other gods also begged Zeus to put an end to the horrendous butchering on the one side and to Priam's sorrow on the other. Zeus sternly agreed. He sent Thetis to her son to persuade him to return to Priam his rival's body, and he sent his messenger Iris to Priam to urge him to go trustingly to the Myrmidons' camp. Hermes would lead him.

So with his chariot loaded with precious gifts for the ransom and some linen sheets to wrap his son's body, the old king left the city at night and, led by Hermes stole unseen into the Greek camp. He reached Achilles' tent where he was sitting

sadly with some of his most loyal friends. Priam then stepped out of the shadow and knelt before Achilles.

'Achilles,' he said, 'think of your Father! Take pity on my grief! Give me back my son! Look,' he added, 'here I kiss the hand that killed him!' And he took Achilles' hand and kissed it. Achilles was astounded to see the old king in his tent. Moreover he was moved by his words and his behaviour.

There was no more anger nor rancour in his heart, but only sorrow and compassion. He whispered, 'Ah! Old man, I can see how much you have suffered! But how could you find the strength to come to my tent alone. You know you have put yourself in mortal danger by coming here. Certainly some god must have helped you. Weep no more Priam. You have no cause for it. Yes you have not come to me in vain, and nor in vain will you have reminded me of my Father. He too, like you, is destined to suffer because my fate is to die under the walls of your

Troy. Don't cry old man, do not grieve any longer!'

After shedding a few tears, the hero raised Priam to his feet. He then ordered his maid servants to wash Hector's body, perfume it and to wrap it in the linens brought by the King of Troy. Going back inside the tent, Achilles said, 'Take your son. Enough tears for now. Come, eat and drink with me, in honour of Hector.'

Whereupon the young hero and the old king both sat at the table facing each other and in great respect of each other. Achilles was strong and brave. Priam was wise and prudent. They were both of equal nobility. At last, Achilles asked, 'How many days will you devote to your son's funeral?'

'We shall mourn him for nine days and on the tenth we shall bury him. On the eleventh we shall have a feast in his honour, then we shall be ready to fight again,' answered Priam.

'Then for twelve days I shall suspend all hostility,' said Achilles in a low voice, and as a sign of loyalty he pressed the old king's hand.

Soon after, Priam sadly mounted the chariot where his son's body had been placed and in the great silence of the night he returned to Troy.

From the top of the tower, his daughter Cassandra recognized him as he approached and shouted, 'Trojans! Come out and see! Hector is returning to his homeland! Come and see!'

They all hastened and the city's gates were opened wide to let in the king's chariot and its sad burden. Hector's body was laid in the centre of a room in the palace. Amid the weeping, the wailing and the lament arrived the beautiful Andromache. She knelt, looked at her husband's livid face and whispered, 'You have died too young Hector, and left me too soon. And with me you have left our son. He cannot yet talk, but Hector, I fear he will never live through his youth now that you are no longer here to defend him.' Andromache wept. By her side old Hecuba and the beautiful Helen wept, and throughout the palace and throughout the town the vast crowd wept.

But Priam ordered, 'Enough now! Bring fire wood for the pyre and you can gather it outside the walls without fear for Achilles has promised to suspend the war for twelve days.'

For nine long days, while the wailing continued, they gathered firewood from the surrounding countryside. They built a gigantic pyre on which Hector's body was finally placed. Then they set it alight. When the last ember of the pyre was put out with wine, the hero's ashes were gathered into a golden urn which, wrapped in purple cloth, was then placed inside a tomb and covered with huge stones. Then, according to

Priam returns to Troy with his son's corpse

*Andromache weeps over
her husband's body*

custom, all assembled in Priam's palace and sat at the funeral banquet.

These were the last honours rendered to Hector, the Horse-Tamer.

Hector's death did not mark the end of the war which was yet to last, and it was not even to end with Achilles death – shot by an arrow from Paris' unerring bow. The destiny of the hero who had chosen a brief but glorious life had followed its course. But Troy still resisted.

Troy was to fall by deceit. It was to fall when the Greeks, accepting Odysseus' advice, pretended they were lifting the siege, and on the seafront where their camp had stood they left a gigantic wooden horse. In that horse (which the Trojans mistook for a divine gift) were hidden the most stalwart Greek warriors. In the still of night they came out of their hiding place and this time there was to be no salvation for the city. The gates were opened and the Greeks sailing back to shore under the cover of darkness, marched into the city inexorably. Massacres and fires marked the end of Troy. Almost all its defenders were killed, Hector's young son was killed, old Priam was killed. But their memory was to last forever like the memory of their victors.

Achilles would be eternally celebrated, and eternally honoured as would be his unfortunate rival Hector who was killed in defence of his homeland and his people.

*The Trojans lead the wooden horse inside the city
walls, thinking it is a sign from the gods*

The
Odyssey

BOOK I

For a long time the Greek princes had beseiged the formidable walls of Troy in Asia Minor. They had fought to avenge the honour of Menelaus, the King of Sparta, and the honour of Greece. Menelaus' wife — the beautiful Helen — had been persuaded by the Trojan prince, Paris, to leave Sparta to live with him in Troy. Their seige lasted ten years until the Greeks finally won. They did not win through strength, however, but only by the shrewdness of one man — Odysseus, King of Ithaca. The story of the Trojan war is told in *The Iliad*.

Leaving the city sacked and burnt, the Greek princes boarded their ships and sailed back to their homeland. Some arrived safely and resumed their thrones, but were betrayed and killed by envious rivals of their crowns. Others, instead of returning home, looked for new countries in distant lands. But ten years after the war, each one of the kings had been accounted for except one: Odysseus. Yet he had left with all the others. But one by one the sails of his ships had disappeared over the horizon and nobody had seen them again.

His people on the rocky island of Ithaca had been waiting for him, but in vain. One, two, three years had gone by. Nothing. More years and still nothing. Was it possible to hope and wait any longer? Or was it wiser to bow one's head to the will of the gods and accept that Odysseus was dead? No. Odysseus was not dead. Living through a thousand adventures, he still yearned for home, although in his heart the hope of seeing Ithaca again grew fainter and fainter. Where was he? Who was he with? Who kept him away? No man knew. The gods knew however, because the fate of men lies in the hands of Zeus, king of all gods.

On Olympus, the home of the gods, Odysseus' protectress Athene pleaded with her father Zeus.

'Ah, Father,' she moaned, 'my heart grieves for Odysseus' fate. He is being held prisoner on a small island in the western sea, by the nymph Calypso, daughter of Atlas, who knows the sea in all its depths and carries on his shoulders the columns that support Heaven and Earth.'

'The young girl is in love with Odysseus,' Zeus replied. 'She keeps him a prisoner, yes, but without violence.'

'But her sweet words, my father, and her tenderness are like chains to Odysseus. He is not happy on Calypso's island, and such is his longing for his rocky Ithaca that he wishes to die. Father, all the kings of Greece are now back in their kingdoms. Why, after ten years, won't you allow Odysseus to return too?'

'My daughter, I am not the one preventing his return! It is Poseidon, Lord of the Seas, who hates Odysseus because he blinded his favourite son, the Cyclops Polyphemus. It is time though that Poseidon gave up his persecution. Ithaca needs a king.'

'Father, may your will prevail,' the blue-eyed Athene said. 'Odysseus is on the island of Ogygia. Send your messenger Hermes to order Calypso to set him free.'

'Ogygia is very far from Ithaca,' observed Zeus, 'and Odysseus has no ship. How will he be able to return home?'

'A raft will do. No-one knows the sea as well as Odysseus.'

After glancing towards the other gods, who nodded in silence, Zeus said, 'Agreed! I shall send Hermes to the island of Ogygia.' A smile lit up Athene's beautiful face. 'And I shall myself go to Ithaca,' she said, 'to Telemachus, son of Odysseus, because there are things happening in Ithaca which fill my heart with anger.'

'What is happening in Ithaca, my sister?' asked Ares the god of war.

'Before leaving for the Trojan war, Odysseus married a very beautiful and wise woman called Penelope. She gave him a son before he left his kingdom. This son, Telemachus, is now twenty years old. Well, seeing that Odysseus did not return, some forty young men, all of noble descent, came forward to ask Penelope's hand in marriage. Whoever marries Penelope shall also acquire the kingdom of Ithaca and all of Odysseus' wealth.'

'I see nothing strange in that,' replied Ares.

'Quite! It is natural for a woman as beautiful, wise and rich as she is to be courted. But the young men who are called the Suitors are behaving in a most unworthy manner. They play the lords and masters in Odysseus' house!'

'And what does Telemachus say? Why doesn't he react?'

'He is only a youth who has never been taught to fight. What could he do against forty men?'

'What about Odysseus' father, Laertes?'

'As Telemachus is too young, so Laertes is too old. He left the palace many years ago and now lives in a peasant's hut in the country.'

'But the people of Ithaca. Why don't they rebel?'

'Because they have lost all hope of seeing their King Odysseus return.'

'And how does Penelope manage to keep the Suitors at bay?' Zeus asked. Athene smiled. 'For some years she has used a trick to elude their request. She started to weave a shroud for Laertes. "When he dies," she said, "I should like my husband's father to be covered by a worthy shroud. When I have finished weaving it, I shall choose from amongst you my new husband." ' The goddess Hera observed, 'It doesn't take years to weave a shroud?'

'Of course not,' Athene replied, 'but Penelope has been undoing at night what she was weaving during the day and so has been able to make her work last. Alas! the Suitors have discovered her trick, and she must now give them her answer. That is why it is necessary to act quickly and allow Odysseus to return to Ithaca.'

Zeus agreed and said, 'Do whatever you must, my daughter.'

Athene begged Zeus to enable Odysseus to return to his homeland.

While Telemachus spoke to Alithene, two great eagles appeared in the sky like a sign from the heavens.

BOOK II

Meanwhile, in the palace of rocky Ithaca, the Suitors had been making merry as usual. They ate, they drank, they talked about Penelope's beauty, they mocked Odysseus whom they thought was, by now, dead, they laughed at Telemachus, they forced old Phemius, Odysseus' minstrel, to play the lyre and sing for them.

They were listening to a ballad when the servants announced to Telemachus that a stranger had arrived. Hospitality was a sacred duty for the Greeks and the young prince therefore hastened to the visitor who was tall, strong and of noble appearance.

'Welcome, friend,' said Telemachus, 'to what was once Odysseus' house. Who are you? Where do you come from?'

'My name is Mentes and I am the son of the Taphian king,' answered the stranger. 'I have come to Ithaca because I used to know Odysseus well and I expected to find him here.'

Lowering his head, Telemachus replied. 'He is not here. He has not returned from Troy. Perhaps his bones are lying on some remote

shore or in the depths of the sea.'

'Perhaps,' Mentes answered, and pointing to the Suitors, he added, 'And who are they?'

'They are the Suitors, vile and insolent people who live off my father's possessions and squander his wealth. They say they want to marry my mother and in the meantime behave as her masters.'

'And you?' To this question Telemachus did not know what to answer and looked down. So with a smile Mentes said, 'It is up to you to act Telemachus. You must go in search of news about your father. Perhaps he is not dead as the Suitors believe. Perhaps he shall return, and if he does, that day will be a day of bloodshed. Go, my young friend. Fit out a ship and go first to Nestor, the wisest of all Greeks. Then go to Menelaus, King of Sparta. I am sure they will both be able to help you.'

'I thank you Mentes, I will do as you tell me. Come now, rest and eat with me'.

But Mentes (who was Athene in disguise) shook his head and said, 'I am sorry, I can't, I must be on my way.' And with those words he vanished, leaving Telemachus full of wonder and fear, but also of hope.

Old Alithene, who knew the art of interpreting the flight of birds and could foretell the future, came to him. He had noticed that the mysterious guest had vanished as if by magic and he asked, 'Who was that man, Telemachus?'

'I don't know,' answered the troubled youth, 'but he gave me good advice. He said that my father might still be alive . . . There!' he exclaimed suddenly, raising his hand, 'look there!' All looked up to the sky. Two great eagles had appeared. Flapping their mighty wings, they descended almost to the ground, and after tearing at each other's necks with their talons, they rose into the sky and disappeared. Impressed, the Suitors remained silent. Wise old Alithene whispered, 'This means Odysseus will come, and he shall do justice.'

While the Suitors resumed their feasting, Telemachus spent the rest of the day pondering over Mentes' words. 'He said his name was

Telemachus' ship sailed from Ithaca.

some of the young men of Ithaca, 'Go to the seashore; you will find a ship. Board it and prepare to sail with Telemachus!'

One by one the youths obeyed and at dusk they found themselves aboard the beautiful ship. Athene took on the appearance of Mentor, an old prophet and friend of Odysseus, and going back to the palace, said to Telemachus, 'What are you doing still here? Your companions are waiting for you. Run to the ship!'

'To the ship?' asked the bewildered youth.

'Yes! Do not linger. Do not waste time telling your mother! Go at once! But beware of the Suitors — they must not know of your departure!'

'But my mother . . .' whispered Telemachus. Mentor shook his head. 'No, there is no time! Go at once and be quick!'

Soon after, the youth ran to the beach where his companions were waiting for him, though not knowing why. He said to them, 'Let's go, my friends. We have a mission to accomplish and we shall do it!'

As the moon rose in the sky, the ship sailed from the island. Soon a light breeze began to blow. Telemachus, who sat at the stern by the rudder, asked Mentor (who was in fact Athene), 'Where shall we go now?'

'To Pylos, where Nestor lives.'

'My life depends on this voyage. I can feel it. It is necessary that I find out something about my father . . . But what will Nestor be able to tell me?'

'Perhaps nothing. But he will certainly be able to give you some good advice. Nestor was the wisest amongst all the Greeks who fought under the walls of Troy. Do not forget it.'

'This stranger who said he was called Mentes', continued Telemachus, 'I think he was a god . . . Well, he also advised me to go to Menelaus.' Mentor replied, 'And so you will. It is the first time you have left Ithaca, the first time you have been to sea and travelled to distant lands, but do not be afraid. I am sure that somebody amongst the gods is assisting you and staying by your side!' Telemachus could not have imagined that at that very moment it was a goddess who was speaking to him. With a good wind filling her sails, the ship voyaged forth on the great sea in which the stars were reflected.

Mentes,' he thought, 'but I don't believe it. No. He was a god and he came to bring me a message. He wanted me to know that my father is not dead. And what have I ever done for him? Nothing! I have remained here thinking I was protecting my mother, but how can I protect her against forty men? It is time for me to leave . . . that god, whoever he was, advised me to go first to Nestor, then to Menelaus. I shall do just that. I shall surely find out something about my father!'

However, not one ship was left to Telemachus since the whole royal fleet had left with Odysseus to go to war. But he had many friends and most of all he had Athene's help. It was she who found a ship and whispered in the ears of

BOOK III

The next day a column of smoke appeared in the far distance. The ship was approaching Pylos, and on the beach a group of people could be seen. Among them a tall, old man with white hair stood out. Pointing to him, Mentor exclaimed, 'That is Nestor, Telemachus!'

Indeed, there on the beach, in front of an altar from which smoke was rising, was wise Nestor who had just performed a sacrifice. Mentor and Telemachus presented themselves to him and he greeted the young men with emotion and affection. 'Welcome, son of Odysseus. You remind me of times long past when there was no sadness. Grief and tragedy were not brought by war, my son, but on our homeward journey. Many of our companions never saw their homes again and some, upon arriving, found death instead of peace. You have come to ask me news of your father Odysseus?'

'Yes. I must find out something about him. My mother is to give her answer to the Suitors who want to marry her . . . and who are squandering our wealth and blackening our honour.'

Telemachus went ashore on the beach at Pylos where Nestor was carrying out a sacrifice.

87

Polycaste — Nestor's prettiest daughter — helped Telemachus to wash and dress.

caste, bathed the prince, rubbed him in perfumed oil and helped him to dress. This was an honour bestowed on guests. Later, a great banquet was laid out. Sipping wine from his golden cup, Nestor declared, 'Yes, Telemachus, it was your father who enabled us to conquer Troy. After ten years of siege and battles, we were still there under the walls and a great many of our best warriors had fallen. Achilles, the strongest of them all, the one who by his mere presence put the Trojans to flight, was dead. He was shot,' the old man went on with a sigh, 'by an arrow from Paris' bow. How could we hope to enter the city after his death? It was then that your father had a wonderful idea. He had a big wooden horse built, so large that our strongest warriors, fully dressed for battle, could hide in the hollow of its belly. Then we took down our tents, dismantled our entire camp, loaded our ships and made believe that we were sailing home. Upon awakening the following morning, the Trojans found that there were no more Greeks, but only a gigantic horse on the beach.'

'I have heard about it,' said Telemachus thoughtfully.

'Your father had foreseen everything. The Trojans dragged the horse inside the walls of the city, and so without a single sword-blow we entered the city that for ten very long years, we had tried in vain to conquer. Odysseus ordered us to wait inside the horse until dark, and when all became silent and the Trojans had gone to sleep feeling so safe that they had not even placed sentries on the walls, your father gave the order and the warriors stealthily came out of the horse's belly.

'Meanwhile, under the cover of darkness our ships turned back. Troy's gates were opened by the warriors from the wooden horse and our army invaded the city. What happened then, everybody knows. The Trojans tried to resist but they were overwhelmed. The city was conquered and set on fire, and Helen, the beautiful Helen, for whom we had fought, was finally returned to her husband Menelaus.

'Telemachus,' added Nestor, 'tomorrow you shall go to Menelaus himself in Sparta, and you will ask his advice. I will give you a chariot and my best horses so that you get there quickly. May it be the gods' will that Odysseus is still alive and able to return to his dear Ithaca!'

'Unfortunately I know nothing of Odysseus. Go to Menelaus,' replied old Nestor, 'and ask for his advice. But before you do, you must spend the night in my palace, because I see from your face that you are weary. And let it not be said,' he concluded, moving away, 'that when Odysseus' son came to me I did not greet him like my own son!'

Soon afterwards, Mentor and Telemachus were welcomed into the stately marble palace. Nestor's loveliest and youngest daughter, Poly-

'I hope so Nestor,' replied Telemachus, 'mostly for my mother who, though she loves my father so, will be forced to marry another man if he does not return!' A solemn silence greeted these words.

Later, as Telemachus lay on his bed, he could not get to sleep. He wondered what would happen in the morning and what advice he would be given by Menelaus. The next day, in a chariot drawn by two splendid white horses, Telemachus and Mentor left Pylos for Sparta — the city famous for its valiant warriors and its beautiful queen.

The journey through the rocky mountains, crested with olive trees, was very pleasant, but Telemachus' heart was heavy with doubt and fear for his father's fate. He hardly dared hope that Odysseus was not dead, that someone was holding him captive in a far-away land and that soon he would be able to return . . .

'What are you thinking about, Telemachus?' asked Mentor suddenly.

'I am thinking that I am twenty, that I have heard much about my father's exploits . . . and that I don't even know him. My friend, I wouldn't recognize him if I saw him now on the road! Isn't that sad?'

They reached Sparta as a feast was being held in Menelaus' magnificent palace. The King was sitting at his table with his friends. The acrobats delighted them with their acts and a bard played the lyre whilst telling ballads of glorious adventures. When he heard that two strangers of noble countenance had arrived in a carriage drawn by two strapping horses, Menelaus ordered his servants to prepare fragrant baths, clean purple tunics and white cloaks for them. It seemed to Telemachus that he was in a fairy-tale world as he was washed, oiled and dressed by the loveliest maid servants. It seemed that he walked in a dream as he crossed the rooms and corridors of the palace. He had never seen a place so rich, so resplendent in gold, marble and ivory.

Telemachus set off for Sparta on a chariot drawn by two splendid horses.

BOOK IV

Telemachus sat at Menelaus' table, and the latter did not even enquire who he was. 'Welcome to Sparta, stranger. Eat and drink with us. You will tell me later if you come to bring me a message or to ask a favour of me. I have fought so much in my life that I want to enjoy some of the sweet things in life now . . .' Menelaus stopped as he saw that young Telemachus gave a start and was gaping at a door which had just been opened. Menelaus turned around and smiled; his wife Helen had just appeared. Helen, the beautiful woman for whom Greeks and Trojans had fought in a terrible war.

Helen stepped forward looking most elegant in her white robe and with her hair gracefully tied back. She came to them with a smile, took her seat by her husband and whispered in his ear whilst looking at young Telemachus. 'I was told of the arrival of two strangers, but we don't know their names . . . I will say something that could be right or wrong, but my heart urges me to speak, Menelaus. I shall tell you therefore that I have never seen somebody so like Telemachus, son of Odysseus, as the young man who sits at your table right now!'

'Indeed, the thought had occurred to me but . . .'

Peisistratus, Menelaus' counsellor intervened: 'Let me tell you, my king, that this is indeed Telemachus son of Odysseus. He has come here to seek your advice. Hear him!'

'Odysseus' son,' Menelaus exclaimed, stretching out his hand to Telemachus. 'This is indeed a fortunate day! The son of a great warrior who, through someone's jealousy has not yet reached his home. What a sad fate for him — the most valiant and the shrewdest of all!'

Hearing these words, Helen began to weep softly. But Telemachus summoned his courage and exclaimed, 'Menelaus, forty men of noble origin but of vile heart are playing lord and master in my father's house. They drink his wine, eat his meat and his fruit. They impudently expect my mother to choose one of them as her husband, and she will be forced to do it — as much as she loves her husband.'

Pale with anger Menelaus replied, 'So some good-for-nothing scoundrel wants to marry your mother? Have faith, Odysseus will come back and do justice!'

'My father is still alive then?'

'He is,' answered Menelaus, 'and I am telling you this, Telemachus, because I have heard it from an old prophet of the sea who knows all its secrets. This old man told me about all the princes who fought with me under the walls of Troy. Some he told me had died, your father he told me lived on an island and was being held by a nymph called Calypso. There Odysseus sheds bitter tears because he longs to return to Ithaca. But he has no ships, no friends, no sailors. However, keep hoping Telemachus, your father will return. When,' Menelaus added, 'I cannot tell. But until then, if you wish, you can stay here in Sparta.'

'Do not ask me to stay in Sparta, O King,' replied Telemachus. 'I would gladly stay even for a year, but I have left my companions as guests of the wise Nestor and my ship at Pylos. How could I abandon them for such a long time?'

'You are right Telemachus. Instead, accept from me some horses as gifts.'

Telemachus smiled. 'I would accept these horses with pleasure if I lived, as you do, in this land of vast plains where it is possible to gallop freely. But my tiny island is not made for horses.'

'This young man thinks wisely,' said Helen. 'He is indeed the son of Odysseus, the shrewdest of all Greeks! In fact,' she went on looking at Telemachus with her large velvety eyes, 'you must know that your father was as brave in battle as he was wise in war conferences.'

So the banquet proceeded and in Telemachus' heart hope was born again. Yes, his father would be back; his father would not only chastise the arrogant Suitors but most of all he would comfort his mother Penelope who had waited, suffered and sighed for so long. That he was on a remote unknown island did not matter, what mattered was that he was alive and until now his return had been prevented. But, thought Telemachus, there must surely be a god who loved him, protected him and would do anything so that he could take to sea again and see Ithaca once more.

Whilst Telemachus was talking to Menelaus, the beautiful Helen appeared.

The Suitors decided to ambush Telemachus on his return to Ithaca.

Meanwhile, in Odysseus' palace, the Suitors had discovered that Telemachus had left. And they were concerned that he had not yet come back. Eurymachus and Antinous, the most authoritative amongst them, called their companions to a meeting. 'Let us not fool ourselves. Telemachus is no longer a boy. We do not know where he has gone, but we can well guess he is searching for news of Odysseus or went to someone for assistance.'

'Assistance for what?' asked one of the Suitors.

'Can't you see? To attack us and chase us out of this house, and perhaps even worse!' exclaimed Antinous. 'He has gone and as far as I know he has taken with him the best youths of Ithaca, the most loyal to him and his father. He will be back, perhaps with allies. We must prevent it. It is necessary to destroy him before he destroys us.'

'What do you suggest we do, Antinous?' asked another Suitor.

'Go to sea and meet him and send him to the devil to keep his father company! There is an ideal place to attack a ship: the straits between Ithaca and the island of Samos. Give me a ship and twenty men and I guarantee that Telemachus will never set foot again in this palace!'

'We should have prevented him from leaving in the first place!'

'Indeed, but it is too late now!'

'Keep calm!' shouted Antinous. 'What are you frightened of? There is still time. Wherever he has gone, the youth will be back and probably without a fleet. His allies, if he has found any, will come later. We must act at once when he least expects it.'

'We all agree!' they shouted. And twenty of them stepped forward ready to carry out Antinous' merciless plot. They lost no time. They went to the port, fitted out a ship and sailed off to lay their ambush.

But Medon, Odysseus' herald, a man still loyal to his far-away king, had overheard the Suitors' conversation, and as soon as Antinous and his companions had gone he went to Penelope and told her everything.

Penelope was terribly upset at the news. She had not been aware of her son's departure. She could not hold back her tears, and turning to her maid servants she reproached them. 'If you knew that Telemachus was about to leave, why didn't you tell me? Perhaps I have lost my husband, and now I shall lose my son as well! What will become of me? Be off with you all! Leave me alone!'

She had thrown herself on her bed sobbing desperately, when Athene appeared to her as a pale ghost. 'Do not weep Penelope', she said. 'Do not fear. Athene will assist you. Be strong.' And with that she slowly vanished.

BOOK V

It was a lovely morning. The sun was shining bright on Ogygia island. Beautiful Calypso was singing and weaving a cloth on her golden spool when Hermes, messenger of the gods, suddenly appeared to her.

'Hermes!' exclaimed the nymph, growing pale. 'Why are you here?'

'Surely you know why, don't you Calypso?' Hermes asked in answer to her question. 'Zeus sent me. I am not happy bringing his message and his order but I must obey him, as you must too. Sweet Calypso, father Zeus wishes you to release Odysseus so that he may return to Ithaca. This is what I have come to tell you.'

Calypso lowered her head and trying to hold back the tears, she whispered, 'Zeus is cruel to me! I love Odysseus and if he goes I shall be forever miserable. But I know,' she added, 'that I cannot disobey. However, Hermes, you must know that I have neither ship nor sailors

to give Odysseus and that I must simply entrust him to the sea. Instead of freeing him I may well be sending him to his death!'

'May Zeus' will be fulfilled,' replied Hermes as he vanished.

Calypso then left her house and walked across the beautiful beach of Ogygia and reached a promontory where she found Odysseus. He sat there scanning the sea with tearful eyes. He did not notice Calypso's presence until she spoke. 'Weep no more Odysseus. You are free to go, if you wish.'

'Free to go?' asked the incredulous Odysseus. Calypso nodded. 'Yes, Zeus has sent me an order. Be brave! Build yourself a raft and I shall provide you with food supplies. Zeus is taking you away from me and it would be pointless for me to cry and hesitate. Go Odysseus, follow your destiny.'

Hermes visited Calypso to tell her that she must release Odysseus.

Calypso remained motionless on the shore, watching Odysseus' raft sail away.

The hero stood up and a new light shone in his eyes. The sea, the raft, Ithaca so remote but not out of reach . . . freedom, home after an absence of twenty years . . . He held Calypso's hands. 'Thank you, my sweet friend, I shall hold you forever in my heart.' Then he began to fell the tallest trees and cut them into rough pieces joining them together and across each other. He cut pine and alder trees, trimmed them with his axe and secured them tightly together. And so in the space of only a few days he had built a big raft with a tree trunk as a mast and a sail rigged on it.

In the meantime the melancholy Calypso prepared his food supplies. When at last all was ready, the two met on the beach for the last time. Everything seemed to favour Odysseus' departure. The sea was calm and glittering, and there was a soft breeze blowing from the west. 'Here Odysseus,' the nymph said handing him a precious tunic, 'put this on. It is worthy of the hero that you are. Wear it in memory of me.'

'Thank you for all you have done for me!'

'Just remember Calypso!'

Odysseus pushed the raft out to sea and hoisted the sail which was immediately filled by the gentle wind; and so he sailed further and further away from Ogygia island. From the shore Calypso watched him go with tearful eyes. She stood motionless looking at him until the raft disappeared on the horizon.

For days and days, Odysseus sailed across the seas on his sturdy raft. After almost three weeks land came in sight. It seemed that the journey was about to end happily . . . but Poseidon, the sea god suddenly noticed him and the fires of revenge blazed in his breast. 'No!' he thundered. 'It will not be so easy for you to reach land Odysseus!' And wielding his trident he unleashed a terrible tempest. The sky, which until now had been clear became so black with clouds that it seemed as if night had suddenly fallen. The calm sea began to stir. Gigantic waves crested with white foam rolled heavily, creating mountains and abysses of water where the raft climbed or sank with a frightful sound of creaking wood.

'What will become of me?' thought Odysseus, clinging desperately to the mast. 'Am I to drown now, just as I thought I was safe at last? Would it not have been better to have fallen while fighting under the walls of Troy?' A wave, more powerful than the others, came hurtling down and scattered the logs of his raft. In a desperate effort Odysseus grabbed one of them and sat astride it. He was like a defenceless twig in the tempest. Odysseus was soon exhausted, but nevertheless he held on for two days. On the third day, when he was about to give up, the wind dropped a little and the sea grew calmer. The waves carried him towards a land covered in forests and glittering rocks. 'I shall be dashed against those rocks,' Odysseus feared. 'My life and my death are suspended between the sea and the land.' But he regained courage and prepared his weary body for yet another struggle. 'If that is where salvation lies, I shall attempt to reach the land.'

Odysseus let go of the log and started to swim towards the coast. A monstrous wave swept him relentlessly against a rock. He quickly grabbed hold of it. Was he safe? . . . No. Another wave pulled him away from the crag, tearing his hands. By now at the limit of his strength, Odysseus swam on looking for a place clear of rocks . . . At last he found one. Yes, there, a river which flowed into the sea. Swimming towards it Odysseus cried with whatever energy he had left in him, 'God of the river! Help me! Whoever you might be! I beg of you!'

The river god heard this desperate prayer and mercifully slowed the current of the river. Gasping, Odysseus swam to the river mouth, leaving behind him the salty water. He continued up the river for a while, and at last felt solid ground under his feet. Moaning and covered in blood and bruises, he stumbled out of the water and falling to his knees, he kissed the ground. He collapsed amongst the reeds of the bank; he tried to get up again but was unable to. After repeated efforts, he succeeded in getting to his feet, and staggered away towards . . .

Poseidon unleashed a frightful storm during Odysseus' voyage.

Nausicaa and her maids were playing.

BOOK VI

. . . Towards what? He did not know where he was. He did not know where to go. He only knew that he was helpless against cold, hunger, weariness and wild beasts, and that he must at all costs find a shelter in which to lie down and sleep. He set off towards some woods where he took shelter under the leaves of a dense shrub. As soon as he lay down, he was overcome by sleep. But after a while (how long he didn't know) he was woken up by the cheerful cries of young girls. Fate had brought Odysseus to the Kingdom of the Phaeacians. On the island where he had set foot stood their city with the palace of King Alcinous, father of young Nausicaa. She was in the full bloom of youth, slender and lithe like a reed and very beautiful. How could Odysseus have imagined that only a few steps from him, princess Nausicaa and her maids were playing? Inspired by Athene, the beautiful Nausicaa had come down to the clear water. Her maids had washed the clothes,

spread them on the grass under the sun, and while waiting for them to dry, they played games together. By Athene's will, the ball with which the girls were playing dropped very near the bush where the tired Odysseus was hiding. 'Whose screams are those I hear?' he asked himself. 'Forest nymphs or women? Where has the sea brought me? Is it a friendly island or a place inhabited by pitiless savages? Whatever it is, I must know.'

Covering himself with some branches he came out of the bush . . . Nausicaa and her maids were running towards it to fetch the ball. At the sight of a man, half-naked, dishevelled, pale and covered with dried salt from the sea, they ran away shrieking in terror. Only one was not frightened and remained — Nausicaa. She stood there quite resolute, full of courage, and faced this wild looking man who had emerged from the woods. She would also have fled with the others had not Athene emboldened her.

96

So Nausicaa waited. Odysseus moved slowly forward staring at her in utter fascination, for it seemed to him he had never set eyes on a more beautiful girl. He wanted to fall at her feet and clasp her knees in a gesture of humility, but standing in front of her, he said, 'I bow to you, Madam. Are you a woman or a goddess? Whoever you are, I beg you to have mercy on me. I have just survived a shipwreck and as you can see I am in want of everything. I have no clothes, no food and I don't even know where I am. I ask only one thing of you — woman or goddess — pity!'

Nausicaa replied, 'Stranger, you are in the land of Phaeacia, whose king is the wise Alcinous, my father. I am his daughter Nausicaa and I can see that you are not an enemy. And you,' she called out to her maids who, full of fright, were peeping and listening from their hiding place in the bushes, 'what are you doing there? Come forward. This man has not come to do us harm but has been washed on to our shores by the sea. He has been shipwrecked and it is our duty to have pity on him. Come, bring what is necessary to wash, oil and dress him.'

Timidly the girls obeyed and Odysseus said to them, 'Leave me, and you too Nausicaa. I shall wash and rub my body in oil and then dress. I am aware of the sorry state in which the sea has left me.' With these words he took the oil and the clothes and went to the river bank where he cleansed himself of the encrusted salt and sand. Meanwhile the maids, with many frightened sighs, said to Nausicaa, 'Let's run away! Can't you see how ugly that man is?'

Odysseus washed himself thoroughly, rubbed himself with oil, dressed in the beautiful tunic that Nausicaa had given him and Athene, assisting him always, endowed him with added good looks. When he reappeared before the young girls, they hardly recognized him as the same man they had beheld earlier. Astonished, Nausicaa whispered, 'Without the help of the gods, my friends, this man would never have reached our island. He looked horrible at first but look at him now. Who amongst us would not take him as her husband?'

'It is true!' murmured the girls in wonder.

'Give him something to eat and drink.' So it was done and as Odysseus at last satisfied his hunger and thirst. Sweet Nausicaa said to him,

'Stranger, whoever you are, you will now come with us to our city. But you cannot ride with me in my carriage. Because if they saw you at my side the Phaeacians would certainly say you were the man I have chosen as my betrothed, and this would neither be true nor proper. Instead you will follow far behind. When you reach the city ask for Alcinous' palace. Enter it without fear and ask for the Queen and King. If you are shipwrecked and wish to return to your home, my mother and father will help you.'

Odysseus spoke to the beautiful Nausicaa.

Having spoken, Nausicaa mounted her carriage and flicking the whip on her white mules, she drove slowly so that Odysseus could easily follow her. When the city came in sight, Odysseus stopped! Nausicaa and her maids went on and soon disappeared amongst the first houses. After a glance towards the white city which stretched along a bay overlooking the blue sea, Odysseus knelt down and turned his thoughts to Athene, for he knew all too well that he owed his life to her. 'Daughter of Zeus,' he whispered, 'hear me. Grant that the Phaeacians may welcome me at the palace and that Alcinous, their king, may receive me with the same compassion that I inspired in Nausicaa.'

Odysseus knelt and paid homage to Athene who had saved him from death.

Then he rose to his feet and continued on his way. And Athene heard him and decided to help him by making him invisible to the Phaeacians, for although they were friendly to strangers, they were always a little suspicious of them. The goddess surrounded his body with a light mist, hiding him from everybody's sight. Odysseus walked ahead along the well-paved roads, along the harbour where several ships were moored and he gazed at the temples close by with their tall white columns. Unaware that he was invisible, he was tempted to ask someone the way, but what would have happened if someone had heard a voice and seen nobody before him? Athene certainly did not want this to happen and that is why she inspired Odysseus to be silent.

Meanwhile, her heart beating fast, Nausicaa had gone back to the palace with her maids who had brought with them the freshly washed clothes.

'What is the matter my daughter?' asked the Queen.

'Nothing, Mother!' replied Nausicaa.

'But you are very flushed in the face!'

'It must be the effort from driving my carriage!' answered the girl, and she ran to her room where she peeped out of her window in her impatience to see again the stranger who had arrived from nowhere and who was as handsome as only a man protected by the gods could be.

Odysseus was still roaming in the city. So many were the stately houses that he could not make out which one was the royal palace. Suddenly he came across a beautiful girl carrying a large wine jar. She looked so refined and her smile was so sweet that he immediately went up to her. 'Gentle maiden,' he said, 'would you lead me to the palace of noble Alcinous? I am a foreigner here. I don't know a single soul . . . and it seems that nobody is taking any notice of me. In fact no-one has so much as even looked at me!' The girl, who was none other than Athene, answered, 'Of course I will stranger. Come with me. Walk in silence and I will show you the way to the palace. Look at no-one, speak to no-one. This is how the Phaeacians are. They do not trust strangers.'

Athene led Odysseus to the palace of Alcinous, king of the Phaeacians.

BOOK VII

Athene set off and the invisible Odysseus followed her to the threshold of a tall palace with marble columns and a huge bronze gate.

'Here, stranger, you have arrived. Go straight in and have no fear, for only bold men are respected. You will find the King and his court at the usual banquet. But first go and pay homage to the Queen whose name is Arete. She has much influence with Alcinous, her husband. If you please her, you can be sure that whatever your request, it will be granted.'

'I have only one request,' answered Odysseus thoughtfully, 'assistance to return to my native land.'

'Then go in with your heart at peace!' said Athene, and she vanished leaving a perplexed Odysseus in front of the magnificent palace gate, its bronze walls ornamented with silver friezes and its doors made of silver and gold. 'If Alcinous is as noble as he is rich,' thought Odysseus, hesitating at the door, 'he will not want to receive a total stranger such as I. Many years have passed since the Trojan War. Of course my name was famous then, but now? Who is Odysseus?'

However, his discouragement did not last. He remembered Athene's advice: 'Enter with your heart at peace!' And so he crossed the threshold of Alcinous' palace.

The Phaeacian princes sat at the banquet table surrounding King Alcinous and Queen Arete like a glittering crown. No one noticed Odysseus approaching, for he was still wrapped in the mist that made him invisible. Crossing the hall, which resounded with cheerful shouts, Odysseus made his way towards the Queen. He was bowing to her when suddenly the mist around him lifted. Utterly astounded, the Phaeacians saw him there, kneeling and stretching out his arm to Arete. A great silence fell over the assembly and Odysseus said, 'Arete, I kneel before you and your husband after long suffering. May the gods grant happiness to you and your guests. As for myself, I beg you to help me to return to my own country, for living so far from it causes me too much grief.'

Having made his request, and according to the custom of the time, Odysseus withdrew slowly as a sign of humility and sat down by the ashes of the hearth. No one dared to speak, they were all still bewildered. Finally old Echeneus, the wisest of the Phaeacians, broke the silence. 'Alcinous, whoever this unexpected guest is, Zeus has certainly sent him. Do not let him sit in the ashes but give him the seat he deserves!'

Alcinous rose at once, took Odysseus by the hand and said, 'Come stranger. You will sit next to me where my favourite son Laodamas sits. He will get up to make room for you.' He snapped his fingers and maids hastened forward with pitchers of perfumed water and a white towel. A place was set for Odysseus, with the most precious dishes. Then Alcinous ordered, 'Fill the cups of all the guests! And after you have drunk my friends, you shall go to the harbour and fit out a ship so that it can be ready to sail off as soon as possible. This man, brought to us by the gods, has asked for our help, so let it not be said that the Phaeacian people have refused to give it to him. Friends and vassals, I shall expect you here tomorrow morning and we shall ask our guest to tell us his story!'

'My story, O King,' replied Odysseus, is a sad one. This I can tell you right away. The gods alone have saved my life. I was shipwrecked on your island, destitute and miserable.'

'Later, my friend. Surely, you must be hungry and thirsty. Start by satisfying those two needs.'

So Odysseus drank and ate, while the guests retired leaving him in the hall with the King and Queen Arete, who always noticed everything. She was the first to recognize the tunic that Odysseus was wearing, and said to him, 'Stranger, I should like to ask you one question first. Who are you and where do you come from? And who gave you those clothes? Didn't you say that you were shipwrecked?'

'Yes, your majesty. I come from very far away, from Ogygia, the nymph Calypso's island in the west. After a long detention there I left on a raft for I was alone there and I had nobody to help me. After a long journey, I had come in sight of this island when Poseidon, who bears a grudge against me, unleashed a terrible tempest. I came out of it by a miracle, swimming to shore . . . These clothes, you ask me? Yes, they come from your palace. In fact the first person who took pity on me and spoke to me was beautiful Nausicaa, your sweet daughter. She gave me something to eat, she had me washed, and told me to come here and beg for your assistance.'

'It was wrong of Nausicaa!' exclaimed Alcinous. 'She should have brought you straight to the palace!'

'It is true,' agreed Arete. But shaking his head, Odysseus replied, 'No, I didn't want to follow her too closely for I respect the King.'

'You speak like a wise man, stranger!' whispered Alcinous. 'How I wish you would never go, but instead remained here, perhaps as our daughter's husband! At any rate I shall keep my promise and no later than tomorrow a ship will take you wherever you wish to go.'

Queen Arete rose and clapped her hands. At once her maids came running. 'Prepare a comfortable bed with the softest and most beautifully coloured sheets. Stranger, you will sleep here under this portico.' Odysseus bowed his head and answered, 'Queen, you do me a great honour. As for me, I could sleep amongst the ashes of your hearth so deep is my respect, and the gratitude I feel for you.'

The King and Queen waited until the maids had brought the bed. Before retiring Alcinous said, 'Tomorrow, if you so wish stranger, you will tell us your name. Sleep now because you certainly need it. Tomorrow the Phaeacians will pay their respects to you and, as I promised you, a ship will be ready to take you to your motherland wherever it might be. Let us leave, my Queen, and let the stranger sent to us by Zeus take the rest he well deserves.' So after the shipwreck and its ordeal Odysseus was at last able to rest in a bed and soothe his tired limbs.

*Odysseus asked for help and protection from the
King and Queen of Phaeacia.*

In the morning there was great agitation in the Phaeacian city. Everyone gathered in the palace square to see and pay their respects to the guest. So that he might inspire everyone with respect, Athene made him look even more handsome, taller and more noble. When he appeared the whispers died down. Everybody gazed at him in admiration.

King Alcinous addressed the crowd. 'Princes and Phaeacian leaders, my people, hear me!

Let it not be said that we do not help those who come to us for assistance. Therefore I command that fifty-two young men go and prepare a ship at once, and be ready to leave. Let the princes and leaders follow me to the palace.'

So while fifty-two young seamen, chosen from amongst the most valiant and worthy, ran to the harbour and rigged a swift ship with a sharp bow, another banquet was being prepared in the palace.

As Demodocus — the blind bard — sang ballads of the Trojan war, Odysseus could not repress his tears.

BOOK VIII

Demodocus the blind bard, strumming on his lyre in order to entertain the guests, chose the Trojan War ballad and started to sing softly. He told of the Greek princes' feats, he told of Agamemnon and Menelaus and Achilles . . . and Odysseus. Hearing his own name and the names of the heroes who for ten long years had shared with him battles and dangers, Odysseus could not withhold his tears and he covered his face with his purple mantle.

He managed to conceal his emotion from everyone except Alcinous who sat next to him. Alcinous then rose and said, 'You can stop your sweet song Demodocus. Let us go to the plain by the sea and show the stranger our skill at games, running, wrestling, jumping and discus-throwing.'

The king led the way and all followed. On the vast plain competitions took place and youths tested their skills against each other — running, jumping and fighting, Laodamas, Alcinous' son, said, 'Let us ask the stranger whether he wishes to take part in the contest! He looks strong and fit enough!'

'Why do you ask me, Laodamas?' asked Odysseus. 'Are you trying to humiliate me?' Then the young and broad-shouldered Euryalus intervened. 'The stranger is right. Can't you see he doesn't look at all like an athlete?'

Odysseus turned to him frowning. 'That, my friend, was a nasty comment,' he retorted. 'It shows that we cannot all have the fortune of combining good looks with wit. An insignificant-looking man may be endowed with great intelligence, whereas another with handsome features may have a deficient mind, like yourself perhaps. You say I am not an athlete. It is true, but I was once. And not amongst the last either. Let us see what I can still do!' And he picked up a stone discus used in competitions, the biggest and the heaviest. He held it, and then with one swing launched it with such force and power that it flew whistling over the amazed Phaeacians and dropped at the far end of the plain. After a minute of astounded silence a voice shouted, 'None of us Phaeacians has ever thrown the discus that far!'

Odysseus then declared in a passion, 'Here I am! Ready to accept any other challenge: racing, jumping, wrestling, archery. Because,' he went on, as everyone assembled eagerly around him, 'I could hit any warrior in battle, even though his companions gathered around to protect him. Philoctetes was the only one to beat me with the bow when we fought under the walls of Troy. The only one!'

They all held their breath. Then Alcinous stepped forward and said, 'Stranger, do not be offended by Euryalus' words. He is young and has no experience and he did not know he was addressing a hero. We all know now that you are a hero even though we don't know your name, and as a hero we want to honour you. Watch the contest that we are about to hold, then when we return to the palace for the feast you will tell us who you are. Remember however, that the fine ship which is to take you back to your homeland is ready.'

Odysseus accepted Euryalus' challenge.

Odysseus smiled. The anger that for one moment had filled his heart and clouded his judgement had vanished. Smiling, he turned to Euryalus. 'Be brave my friend,' he said. 'Show me what you can do!'

'I shall, stranger,' replied the young man. 'But first accept this gift from me as a token of our reconciliation.' And he handed Odysseus a sword studded in silver and with a sheath of ivory. Odysseus thanked him. Then sitting by Alcinous' side he watched the contests between the young Phaeacians.

By nightfall Alcinous and his court had returned to the palace for the feast. There Odysseus met Nausicaa again. It seemed that she had been waiting for him. 'Be happy stranger. When you are back in the land of your fathers, do not forget me.'

'When I am back in my country, Nausicaa, not a day shall pass without my remembering the gratitude I owe you.'

The new banquet began and the blind bard Demodocus again sang about the Trojan War. Once more, on hearing about the war, Odysseus could not suppress his tears and Alcinous, putting down his cup asked him, 'Stranger, tell me why you weep? Perhaps a brother or a friend of yours died under the walls of Troy?'

In the great silence which had settled on the assembly, Odysseus replied, 'Alcinous, glory of your people, I shall tell you why I weep. And I shall tell you the strange adventures I have lived through. I shall also tell you who I am for it is fair that you should know. Yes,' he went on, 'I have lost a great many friends under the walls of Troy, that is why I weep when I hear of their exploits. I fought by their side. I am in fact Odysseus.'

Alcinous invited Odysseus to tell them of his adventures.

A gasp of wonder rose from the guests when these words were heard. And Odysseus continued, 'I live on the island of Ithaca which to me is the most beautiful land on which the sun has ever shone. Since the end of the Trojan War, I have been trying to return there. You see Alcinous, when the beautiful city of Troy was besieged and set on fire, and when Helen was finally set free and the war was ended, we Greeks embarked on our homeward journey. I led my fleet of warriors from Ithaca. On our way we attacked Ismarus, city of the Cicones, and we sacked it in order to get fresh food supplies. But instead of obeying my orders, which were to return to the ship immediately, my men stayed in the city and got drunk. When the Cicones counter-attacked, many of my men were killed. With great difficulty we got back on the ship and fled.

'We encountered a storm which scattered our fleet. We had to lower our sails so that the wind would not rip them. After three days the clear weather returned and the sun shone again. But we were off course. As we passed Cape Malea we could not make headway against the currents which, for nine days, carried us further and further west. On the tenth day we found land. There was a city in sight and I sent three messengers to say that we came in peace. Alas, it was the city of the Lotus-Eaters, whose inhabitants eat no meat, only the fruit of the lotus plant. Those of my men who ate the fruit lost their minds, forgot who we were and forgot their country. We had to use force and bind them like enemies to bring them back to the ships. Again we fled.

BOOK IX

'Still shaken, we reached the land of the Cyclopses who live in deep caves or on top of mountains. We moored our twelve ships in the bay of an adjoining island and I went ashore to hunt with my men. On the following day, leaving the rest of my fleet, I took my ship to the land of the Cyclopses because I was eager to find out more about them. From the sea we saw the opening of a vast cave and an enclosure for animals nearby. Taking with us gifts for the Cyclops as well as a full jar of wine, we went ashore on that wild and beautiful land. There was no-one about. We entered the deserted cave. There were freshly-made goats' milk cheeses, stacked on racks, and my companions took many. Then they said, "Let us leave now Odysseus, let us return to the ship!"

'Ah, if only I had listened to them. "No," I answered, "let us remain. I want to find out who lives in this cave." And so we remained and we ate, and when we had eaten we heard a great crash. It was the Cyclops who had returned and dropped a great load of dry logs. He herded his flock of sheep and goats inside the cave and then closed the entrance with an enormous boulder. Then he began to milk his goats. He was a hairy giant who had in the middle of his forehead just above his nose, one shiny, evil eye. Imagine our terror when he suddenly fixed it on us!

' "Who are you strangers?" he asked when he saw us, I stepped forward and replied, "We are Greeks arrived here by chance and we ask for your hospitality!"

'To our horror, the Cyclops, in reply, stretched out his hand, grabbed two of my men, dashed them against the ground and ate them up! I thought of attacking him with my sword, but I didn't, knowing how pointless it would have been. My sword would have been very little against such a giant! We all huddled terrified in a corner and spent the night like that, while the Cyclops snored, filled with food.

Odysseus handed Polyphemus a jar of wine in order to make him drunk.

At dawn he woke up, stretched out his hand once more and catching another two of my men, killed and ate them. And the same thing happened again in the evening when he returned to the cave, having blocked it from the outside during the day.

'Then I came forward with the jug of wine and said, "Now you have eaten, you must drink, Cyclops!" The Cyclops took the jug with his gigantic hand and drank a great gulp of the wine. "Good wine, stranger," he said, pleased. "Give me some more!" So I did and he drank three times.

'Not used to such strong wine he became drunk very quickly and his head began to nod. "Tell me, what is your name," he mumbled, "so that I may give you a present?"

' "My name?" I answered. "Yes, I'll tell you what my name is. My name is Nobody. Now tell me, what is your present?" He gave a great yawn, stretched on the ground and, sniggering, he continued, "I shall eat you last. That will be my present!"

'Drunk as he was, he fell asleep immediately. Then I turned around to my friends and said, "Quick, we must save ourselves! We cannot get out of here as we will never move the boulder from the exit. But grab that pole and sharpen it with your swords. I shall stir up the fire!"

Without asking questions they obeyed and soon we had a long pole which looked like a giant spear. I had put more logs on to the fire, which was now burning like a brazier. On the blazing fire I heated the tip of the pole until it was red and smouldering. Then I said, "Come with me. Let us avenge our friends who have been killed and eaten, and let us escape!"

'And so we thrust the red-hot pole into the Cyclops' closed eye. He gave an horrendous howl. He got up holding his bloody eye and hurled the pole away while we escaped to one corner of the cave. He staggered, howling and moaning, then he began to shout, "Brothers! Brothers! Help! They are murdering me! Help! . . ." and he paced the cave, blind and mad with pain and rage. Soon after, voices were heard outside. The other Cyclopses had come, and they asked, "Polyphemus," for that was the Cyclops' name, "why are you screaming so? What has happened to you?"

' "Nobody is killing me!" answered the Cyclops. And so his brothers said to him, "If Nobody is hurting you, you must be drunk and dreaming, Polyphemus! Ask your father Poseidon to help you!" And they went away.

'Polyphemus called them desperately for a long time, complaining that Nobody had blinded him. The terrified animals were bleat-

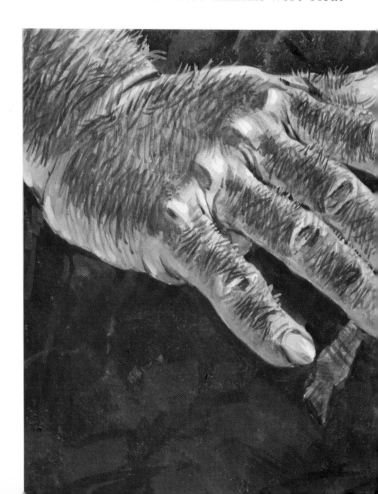

Odysseus and his companions escaped from Polyphemus' cave by clinging under the sheep's belly.

ing uncontrollably and the whole cave echoed with various wild screams. At last the ghastly night passed. But at dawn, Polyphemus stood by the entrance, from which he had removed the boulder, and held his fingers like a gate to stop us from going out with the animals. What was to be done? How were we to get out? I had an idea suddenly. We hitched the sheep together in threes, with ropes, and each man grabbed hold of the long strands of wool under the middle sheeps' belly. I hung on under the belly of a ram, and so we moved towards the exit. The giant passed his hand over the back of each beast but not under its belly and thus all my companions were able to get out of the cave . . .

'I came last. And Polyphemus, groping the back of the ram under which I clung, mumbled. "Ah, my ram, how come you are last this morning, when you are always the first to be out. Perhaps you are sad because your master has been blinded? But I shall catch Nobody and when I have him I shall wreak a terrible vengeance on him!"

'So saying he pushed the ram outside the cave and I was free. We let go of the sheep and ran to the ships, loading on to them many sheep, and as my companions wept for the loss of our friends I shouted, "Do not cry, but think of your lives! To your oars and let's get out of here!" Soon after when we were far enough from the shore I shouted, "Polyphemus, you have killed innocent people and you have received the punishment you deserved for it!" As an answer the enraged Cyclops hurled a boulder into the sea, creating great waves. "If you are asked who blinded you, you can answer that it was Odysseus, son of Laertes!"

'And we left while Polyphemus continued to hurl boulders in our direction, trying to overturn our ships or hit us. But the wind filled our sails and we sailed away fast. In the end Polyphemus stopped hurling rocks and knelt down on the beach. Raising his hands to the sky he moaned, "Poseidon, my father, hear me! Look what Odysseus, son of Laertes, has done to me! If you love me, punish him by preventing him from reaching his home. And if it is written that he must return, make him suffer on the sea; make him lose all his companions; and when he finally reaches his home may he only find misfortunes there!"

'We sailed all day, roasting lamb and eating and drinking heartily. But in spite of all, our hearts were heavy as we remembered our dear friends so brutally killed.

BOOK X

'We sailed for several days until we reached the island of Aeolus, the home of Aeolius, Lord of the Winds, who lived in a vast palace with his six sons and six daughters and where lavish banquets were laid every day. He was very generous to us, and bestowed upon us his royal hospitality. He was eager for news about the Trojan War and when, after one month, I asked him permission to leave, he said to me, "You may leave, Odysseus, and since you are my friend, I give you this leather pouch as a gift. In it are enclosed all the winds of the tempest. Beware you do not open it or you will come to grief. I have left only one wind free, Zephyrus, who is favourable and will take you all the way to Ithaca. Farewell!"

'And so we left with Zephyrus blowing us homeward. I was standing at the helm with the pouch containing all the tempestuous winds tightly shut before me. I was at peace. Soon I spied the shape of Ithaca my beloved country. I could see its fires glowing in the night. The journey was coming to an end. But I am only a man, I became tired, my eyes closed and sleep, which is usually a blessing, this time came only to strike me a cruel blow.

'As I slept one of my sailors said to his companions, "Who knows what treasures Aeolius has given Odysseus! Just think! After years at war we poor devils are returning home empty handed, while Odysseus brings with him this pouch which is certainly full of gold! Come on, let's open it and share the booty!"

'And so the wretched men opened the pouch. At once the winds of the tempest came out howling, hissing and infuriated. They whirled round the ships and the sea suddenly swelled with dark waves which swept us far away, dashing us and ripping the sails.

'We could not even steer — we were dragged away and when, after I know not how many days of storm, land came to sight, we did not even know where we had come to. We drifted into a natural harbour, tightly enclosed amongst overhanging rocks and sheltered from the stormy seas. A good place certainly, but where were we? I sent some of the men to explore the area. To our misfortune we discovered we had come to the land of the Laestrygonians, one of the most cruel and warlike peoples that I have ever met.

'They showed their ferocity immediately. When the exploring party arrived in their village, they were assaulted, captured and one of them was killed and eaten. They were cannibals . . . The others escaped and returned to the ships frightened out of their wits. I gave the order to loosen the sails at once and to row with all our might in order to get away from the island as quickly as possible. But, as I said, the fleet had taken refuge in a natural cove with overhanging cliffs. And from the top of these cliffs the Laestrygonians began to throw rocks. It was a terrible hail of stones which shattered ships, knocked down men, and broke masts. Some of my companions jumped into the sea, trying to save themselves by swimming ashore. They were seized and slaughtered. As my fleet was destroyed I escaped with great difficulty . . .

Odysseus' ship sailed from the island of Aeolia towards Ithaca.

'Out of twelve ships only one remained! The other eleven were lost and so were their crews. What was I to do? What indeed? Devastated as we were, we took to sea once again. We abandoned ourselves to the winds, which after several days blew us to an island called Aeaea. There, as though a god were guiding us, we entered a calm bay and spent a quiet night.

'At dawn I took my spear and my sword and went to explore by myself. I climbed over rocks and walked through woods and in the distance I saw smoke rising. It came from a house hidden in dense woods. I thought I would come back later to see who lived in it, and in the meantime I returned to the ship, killing on my way a great stag which we roasted and ate heartily.

Circe turned Odysseus' companions into pigs.

' "Friends," I said as we were eating, "I saw a house in the forest. We must go there. But let us be cautious. We shall divide into two groups. I shall lead one and Eurylochus shall lead the other. One will go to the house while the other remains here. We shall draw lots to decide which group will go." It fell to Eurylochus and his group to go and explore. He left with his men . . . and came back alone much later, running and mad with terror, unable to speak.

'Stuttering with fright he could barely tell me what had happened. In the house they had found a beautiful witch goddess called Circe, who offered them a lavish meal. All had eaten but him, Eurylochus, who felt uneasy. In fact, his companions had barely finished their meal when Circe touched them one by one with her wand and changed them all into pigs! "Into pigs Odysseus! They are not men anymore, do you understand? They are animals! Circe is a witch! Let us flee," Eurylochus said, "while there is still time!" and he wept as he spoke.

'But I said to him, "No! We cannot abandon our companions. Wait for me here!" Then dressed and armed for battle, I set off towards the house of the witch goddess. On my way I met a handsome youth whom I recognized as Hermes, a god who has always favoured me. He said to me, "Beware Odysseus! You are on your way to free your friends from the magic spell, but the spell can also be cast on you. As soon as Circe offers you something to drink unsheath your sword and threaten her with death. It will be the only way to save yourself."

Odysseus and his friends were Circe's guests for one year.

With these words, Hermes vanished and I reached Circe's house. I was greeted by meek lions and wolves, which were in fact men turned into beasts by the witch goddess. I walked past them without coming to any harm and went into the house.

'Circe came to meet me. She was extraordinarily beautiful, and with a smile she said "Whoever you are, stranger, you are welcome. Here," and she had a maid bring me some wine, "drink this and refresh yourself." I took the cup that she was handing me, but instead of raising it to my lips I threw it down on the ground and drew my sword, holding Circe by her arm and threatening her with death. Pale as a sheet, she screamed, "Ah! Who on earth are you? Why haven't you drunk? Why haven't you turned into a pig? Why have you resisted my magic spell? Are you perhaps Odysseus? I knew that Odysseus was coming . . ."

' "Yes Circe, I am Odysseus," I replied, "and if you want to save your life, give me back my companions!"

' "I want to be your friend Odysseus!"

' "Do you really Circe?" I said. "Then give me back my companions!"

' "You will have them back, for I do not want to go against the will of the gods!"

'She went into the pigsty and raising her wand she ordered the pigs to become men. And there reappeared all my companions. They saw me and embraced me in deep gratitude. Circe laid out for us a great banquet which we all enjoyed without fear of being bewitched again. We remained guests of Circe for about one year. Finally we decided to leave and when the beautiful witch goddess heard of our decision she said: "Go Odysseus because this is how it must be. But beware, before setting foot on Ithaca, you shall have to wait a long time still. Come, I shall reveal to you some of the things that will happen to you during your journey, because I can foresee the future . . . "

'She told me many things which did come true and of which I shall speak later. Things that frightened me so much that I exclaimed, "What will become of me Circe! I fear the future already! What life, what death will I encounter?"

' "I cannot tell you that. You will have to go to Hades, Kingdom of the Dead, and consult the prophet Tiresias. He will be the one to reveal these facts to you."

' "How will I reach the Kingdom of the Dead?"

' "Take your ship to the edge of the world where the Acheron river flows into the sea. You will recognize the beach for it is dominated by a very tall cliff. When you are there, dig a hole and make sacrifices to the gods. When it is done, turn to the river and you shall see the souls of the departed."

'Thus spoke beautiful Circe, and so with my companions, I set off on a new journey towards the unknown.'

BOOK XI

'So to the ship we went, taking with us, as well as supplies, a ram and a black ewe to sacrifice on the beach of Hades. By Circe's kindly spell a favourable wind blew us throughout the whole day.

'At last we reached the brim of the ocean and came in sight of the Cimmerians' land, wrapped in a perpetual dark fog so that night seemed to last eternally. This was the place we were searching for. We moored our ship and stepped ashore taking with us the two animals. Making our way along the calm, lapping ocean, we reached the spot Circe had described. While Perimedes and Eurylochus held the victims, I drew my sword and dug a hole about a cubit wide and a cubit deep. I paid homage to the dead, first with milk and honey then with sweet wine and finally with water. I sprinkled the earth with white flour and promised that as soon as I got back to Ithaca, my motherland, I would carry out more and richer sacrifices. I sacrificed the two animals, slashing their throats so that the black, hot blood fell into the hole. It took but a few moments and to my amazed eyes the souls of the dead came crowding up to me, moaning incessantly. I was filled with horror and quite unconsciously I unsheathed my sword and threatened them as though it could have harmed them!

'They stepped back nevertheless and I looked for Tiresias amongst them, for I had to question him alone. At first I could not see him, but then I spotted him. There he was holding a golden sceptre. When I greeted him he said to me, "Divine Odysseus, why have you forsaken the sunlight for this mirthless place? Step away from that hole and put away your sword. I shall drink the victims' blood and then I shall speak to you."

'I stepped back and after drinking the blood he said, "Radiant Odysseus, you are seeking your way home but a god will make it very difficult for you. You shall not escape the persecution of Poseidon whose favourite son you have blinded. Nevertheless, if you act cautiously you will succeed. What matters now is that you do not harm the Sun god's cattle. You will find his cows grazing on the green fields of Thrinacie. Beware! If you harm them there will be no pity on you or your ship. You Odysseus," he went on, "will not die. You will reach your homeland but you will find your palace invaded by strangers courting your wife and squandering your wealth. Those arrogant nobles will be eager to take your place. You shall grow very old and you shall die at sea. More I cannot tell you!"

When he reached the place described by Circe, Odysseus dug a hole with his sword and began the sacrifices.

' "These things, Tiresias, have been decided by the gods and we cannot oppose them. But tell me, amongst the souls I can see the ghost of my mother. How will she recognize me?"

'Moving away, Tiresias replied, "Any ghost to whom you give the blood to drink will speak to you in a sensible manner. Those you reject will retire. Farewell, Odysseus!" Then with much grief in my heart I stood waiting for my mother's soul to come to the hole and drink the dark blood.

'As soon as she drank she recognized me and drawing nearer to me she said moaning, "My son, how did you come here? . . . You are alive! . . . Why are you not in Ithaca?"

' "Mother," I replied, overcome by emotion, "I have not yet returned to my rocky Ithaca and I am here because I needed to speak to Tiresias in order to learn something about my fate. But you mother, how did you die? Suddenly or after a long illness? Was it perhaps grief from my long absence that brought you here? . . . Can you tell me of my father, of my dear son whom I left behind as a mere child? And can you tell me of my wife Penelope and of her feelings? Has she been faithful to me or has she remarried?"

' "Oh no! Penelope is faithful to you and spends her nights and days weeping. Your son lives as a young prince should live and nobody, until now, has taken anything from him. Your father, however, lives in the country like a miserable peasant and is wasting away thinking of you, forever absent! As for me . . . Oh my son, I died of grief because you did not return."

'I tried to embrace her. Three times I opened and closed my arms but three times I clasped nothing but thin air. "Alas Mother, why do you avoid me," I said, "when I want to embrace you?"

' "I am not avoiding you," she answered. "What is left of me is only my soul, my ghost, which you cannot touch or feel anymore!"

'As we talked, more ghosts came and gathered round the hole wanting to drink the blood of the victims. Drawing my sword I threatened them, allowing them to drink one by one only. They were mostly women and they told me their stories . . . " '

At this point Alcinous interrupted Odysseus and asked him, 'Tell me, divine hero, whilst you were down there in the gloomy Kingdom of the dead, did you see any of your comrades who fell under the walls of Troy?'

'I did,' answered Odysseus. 'I did indeed.' Then he resumed his tale.

'Suddenly while the women disappeared, Agamemnon's soul approached. He was the supreme commander of all the Greek troops at the siege of Troy. He drank the blood,

recognized me and stretched out his arms to hug me. But all the vigour had gone from his limbs. Moved and weeping I asked him. "Agamemnon, illustrious king, how did you come here? Perhaps you died at sea? Perhaps you fell to some hostile tribe on whose land you set foot on your return from Troy?" Pale and full of sorrow, Agamemnon replied, "No Odysseus! I was murdered in my own house! It was my wife who killed me! Thus she welcomed me after ten years of absence!"

'More souls were approaching. There came the soul of the great Achilles, of his dear Patroclus, of Ajax the hero who feared nothing in battle. Achilles recognized me and said, "Ah, Odysseus! You mad man! What trick have you used to make your way to this sombre place?"

' "Achilles, strongest warrior amongst all Greeks, I came here to ask Tiresias some questions. I see that in the same way you dominated everybody during your lifetime, so you do in death as well! You are the king here!"

' "No," he answered sadly, "no. I would rather serve a master, be a destitute wretch and be alive, than king of all these dead people. But let us talk about my son Neoptolemus. How is he? Is he behaving as he should?" I told him that indeed his son had distinguished himself fighting ahead of everyone in the siege of Troy,

and that although he was always on the front line he had never been wounded. Achilles smiled and showed his contentment. Then with great strides, he left.

'I saw the other ghosts and all spoke to me except Telamonian Ajax whom I had greatly annoyed because Achilles' weapons were given to me and not to him. Seeing him standing aloof and looking the other way, I said to him, "Ajax, even in death you still hold a grudge against me?" He gave no answer and walked off without a glance. From a distance I heard his voice full of anger.

'I also saw there Minos, son of Zeus and king of the dead. I saw the giant Orion carrying a massive club with which he hunted wild beasts. I saw Tantalus standing in a pool of fresh water which vanished as he tried to drink it. Above him dangled shiny fruit, but when he tried to grasp one the wind blew them high up into the sky. I saw Sisyphus who pushed a heavy boulder to the top of a hill and everytime he was about to reach its crest, the boulder escaped him and came rolling down again to level ground, so that once more he had to push it up . . .

'I saw many more souls, but horror overcame me in the face of this multitude of howling ghosts and I ran back to the ship.

Odysseus approached his mother's ghost in the Kingdom of the Dead.

Odysseus heard the song of the Sirens.

BOOK XII

'So off we sailed again. As the ship ploughed through the blue sea I remembered Circe telling me we would encounter the rocks inhabited by the Sirens. "The Sirens' voices," Circe had said, "bewitch any man who hears them and makes him forget everything and all that is dear to him. Remember, their songs are the sweetest music, but if you should listen to them you will be enticed to your death! As you sail near the rocks, tell your companions to plug their ears with beeswax. And if you wish to listen to the music yourself, have them tie you to the ship's mast."

'This is what we did when we saw the two rocks appear on the horizon. Bound to the mast I heard the sweetest songs of the Sirens who called me and invited me to join them and such was my desire to do so that I shouted in a frenzy, "Release me! Release me!" But unable to hear me or the Sirens because of the beeswax in their ears, my companions tightened the ropes around me. Thus I escaped the sweet but deadly magic of the Sirens.

'We sailed away quickly from those enchanted and dangerous rocks and when I could no longer hear even the echo of the Sirens' songs I gestured to my men to remove the wax from their ears and to untie me.

'Suddenly, however, the sea became rough. We could hear a rumbling growing louder and louder, while a cloud of black smoke filled the sky, darkening the sun! Terrified, my men dropped their oars and the ship was brought to a standstill. "Friends," I said, "We have lived through many dangers before, haven't we? I don't know what this noise means but it can't be any worse than the Cyclops whom we beat. Be brave! To your oars again and you, helmsman, hold steady the steering oar! Forward! We do not fear the sea!"

'They obeyed me but I trembled in my heart for I knew that the roar, the agitation of the waters and the smoke, all indicated that we were approaching the most dangerous place in the seven seas. We were about to pass between Scylla and Charybdis!

The dreadful passage between the caves of Scylla and Charybdis.

'Circe had told me of Scylla and Charybdis. We sailed close to the coast and up a channel — my companions rowed on but were frightened by the roar and the fog that from time to time fell upon us, then lifted again. "You will pass through a strait overlooked by two gaping caves," Circe had said. "In the first one lives the terrible Scylla that barks relentlessly, like the shrill yelp of a bitch. It is a horrible monster with twelve feet and six necks! In the second cave lives Charybdis, another sea monster which sucks in sea water three times a day and then spits it back out again. Odysseus, beware not to be there while it drinks!"

'We pressed forward and there appeared on the right and on the left the two enormous cave mouths. We were staring at Charybdis when Scylla darted out from its lair and grabbed six of my men, the strongest and most skilled, and threw them down into the sea. I turned around grasping my spear, but too late. I saw amongst the waves arms and legs and I heard the screams of the poor devils who called out my name. Irresistably they were drawn into the mouth of that horrendous cavern and disappeared.

'We managed to proceed without further damage, and soon after we came to a calm expanse of sea. In it appeared Thrinacie, the Island of the Sun. From the ship we could see vast green fields where long-horned cows were grazing. I told my companions, "Friends, Tiresias warned me to keep clear of this island, the Island of the Sun. Better to avoid it and continue on our journey homeward."

' "We are tired Odysseus," replied Eurylochus, "and so are you. We cannot go on in this condition. Let us go ashore and rest awhile. Nothing will happen that we cannot handle."

'We went ashore therefore. The place was lovely and soon sleep overcame me. "I have listened to you, friends," I said. "Let us rest then. I give you one order only — do not harm the sacred cows of the Sun god."

' "Sleep Odysseus and trust us," they answered, and I fell asleep.

'While I slept Eurylochus fetched the spears, gave them to the men and, stupidly, they all went hunting. They slaughtered many cows, the fattest ones. They carried them onto the beach, skinned them, roasted them and started feasting. I was asleep and unaware of what had happened. But upon waking I smelt roasting meat and with a terrible feeling of misfortune I ran to the ship. "What have you done?" I shouted. "Now Zeus' revenge will strike us!"

'But it was too late by then, much too late! Indeed, on Mount Olympus, the sun god Hyperion, whose cows were sacred, had turned angrily to Zeus and complained, "Odysseus' companions have killed my cattle! I call upon you to punish them or I shall leave the sky and go down to Hades and shine among the dead!" Zeus replied, "I shall punish them myself with my lightning."

'And so it was. After a few days we left the island and were sailing towards the not too distant Ithaca when suddenly the blue sky became overcast with clouds and it rapidly grew darker. Amongst the clouds there were great flashes of lightning and while the waves heaved fiercely, a bolt of lightning struck our ship. There was a blinding flash, a breaking sound and the mast crashed down while the ship whirled madly on the waves. My terrified crew were flung screaming overboard and vanished under the water. I found myself amongst the waves gasping for air. I spotted a floating log and clung to it with all my energy. Waves and wind swept me inexorably back towards the caves of Scylla and Charybdis. On the rock which jutted out over the lair of Charybdis, I caught sight of a fig tree which had massive roots. With a desperate leap I caught it and hung to it whilst three times, with a terrible roar, the monster sucked in water and the wreckage of my ship. After the third time I threw myself back into the sea and swam towards a piece of wreckage, sat astride it and started paddling with my hands. For nine days I drifted aimlessly. On the tenth night I reached the island of beautiful Calypso. The rest of the story, you already know.'

And so ended Odysseus' tale. Alcinous then spoke. 'Odysseus,' he said, 'you have suffered much. But your troubles are over, for now you will return to Ithaca. The ship awaits you in the harbour. The crew is the most skilled amongst the Phaeacians. Let us drink then and make offerings to Zeus. Tomorrow night you will leave!'

Odysseus managed to cling to a piece of wreckage and saved himself.

116

Having reached Ithaca, the Phaeacians carried the sleeping Odysseus ashore and placed their gifts around him.

BOOK XIII

For Odysseus the following day was a very long one. Continually he turned his eyes to the harbour where he could see, swaying on the water, the ship that was to take him to Ithaca. The Phaeacians' gifts were already loaded on to it. Alcinous though was in no hurry to dismiss his famous guest. The banquet was followed by sacrifices which were followed by another banquet. At the end of this Odysseus rose from his chair and said, 'Alcinous, and all of you my friends, may you live long and happily and may the gods keep you and your generous people from harm. And,' he added, 'may I see my dear wife again!'

The cups were then filled for the last toast. Odysseus wished happiness to Queen Arete and, preceded by a herald and followed by slaves who carried cloaks, tunics, bread and wine, he moved towards the ship. Deeply moved, he boarded the ship. The sailors took their places at the oars to manoeuvre the vessel out of the harbour, as the sun was setting and the stars began to appear in the sky. Odysseus was tired, not from effort, but from sheer emotion. He felt he was setting off on the last phase of his never-ending voyage. He lay down on a mantle and fell asleep.

He was in a deep sleep when the Phaeacians, out of the harbour, hoisted the sails. He went on sleeping while the sharp bow of the ship steadily cut her way through the waves. Still he slept, when over in the light of dawn there appeared the craggy shape of Ithaca. On Ithaca there was a quiet cove, a small natural harbour where the water was crystal clear. There the Phaeacians moored and, without waking Odysseus they carried him ashore in their arms and settled him down under an age-old olive tree. Around him they stacked their gifts and then they left.

They were, alas, going towards a sad fate. In fact, Poseidon, who saw what they had done, rushed to Zeus. 'Father of all the gods,' he exclaimed, 'I cannot tolerate the fact that Odysseus has reached his homeland whilst sleeping peacefully amongst so many gifts, carried there as a triumphant king. I ask for revenge!'

'Take it then!' answered Zeus. So as the ship was about to reach the Phaeacian island a terrible thing occurred. The sailors had already lowered the sails and started to row into the harbour. From the shore friends and companions were already waving signs of welcome, when suddenly the ship and its crew were turned into a massive black rock!

In the meantime, in Ithaca, Odysseus had woken up. He could see nothing but mist around him. In dismay he said, "Where am I? Surely not in Ithaca. There was never such dense fog on my island! Where then? Where did the Phaeacians leave me? Have they betrayed me? No, for all around me are their gifts. So? . . . ' Muttering to himself and with a heavy heart he roamed about in the fog, until he saw a shepherd in the midst of it. 'Tell me my friend,' he asked at once, 'where are we? What is the name of the land we tread on?'

'This is the island of Ithaca,' replied the shepherd.

'Ithaca . . . I have heard of it. I come from Crete. I have fled from there for I have been accused of murdering a man. A Phaeacian ship brought me here. While I slept the sailors carried me ashore and left.' The shepherd smiled and turned into a tall, beautiful and majestic lady. She was in fact Athene, who wanted to put him to the test.

'Odysseus, you would indeed be too cunning if you had succeeded in deceiving even me! I am Athene, daughter of Zeus.'

'Goddess, it is difficult to recognize you when you take on the appearance of a humble shepherd! I give you my thanks, O divine lady, and I beg you to give me proof that we are really in Ithaca!'

'Look!' said Athene.

The mist was lifting and Odysseus saw his beloved land. He knelt on the ground and kissed it, deeply moved. But the goddess said, 'Come, come Odysseus, do not waste time. Hide the Phaeacian gifts in this cave, and think about what you must do because if you should go to the palace at once the Suitors would find it easy to slit your throat!'

'And so I would meet the same end as poor Agamemnon who was killed when he returned home!' muttered Odysseus, and he added, 'How must I behave towards the Suitors, pray tell me? I fear no-one if you are near me.'

Having woken up, Odysseus asked a shepherd where he was.

118

'I shall not leave, especially when you will have to take up arms to avenge yourself and do justice as well. Do not fear. But now you are alone and they are many. You must, therefore, act very cautiously. Whoever sees you will recognize you.'

'What should I do then?'

Athene smiled. 'I will be by your side, Odysseus, never far from you. I will start by making you unrecognizable to anyone. I shall make your skin wither, your hair become white and matted and I shall dim your sharp eyes. You will look repulsive to all, Odysseus, even to your own wife who loves you and has never ceased to wait for you. First of all,' Athene went on, 'you will go and look for Eumaeus, the swineherd who looks after your pigs and who has remained loyal to you. You will find him by the Raven's crag beyond the spring of Arethusa.'

'Eumaeus! Then he is still alive?'

'He is indeed, and he will be able to help you a great deal.'

'But,' asked Odysseus, 'what about my son?'

'He is in Sparta at the court of Menelaus. He went there in the hope of finding news of you.'

'So far! O divine lady, perhaps he too will suffer what I have suffered on the sea! . . . '

'No. I shall go to him at once. I will order him to come back . . . In fact,' Athene added, 'the Suitors have laid an ambush and are ready to attack his ship. But I will see to it that their evil plot does not succeed. If blood must be shed it shall be their own.'

With these words, Athene touched Odysseus with her wand. At once the hero turned into a miserable old man. His skin withered, his bright, strong eyes grew small and bleary; she threw a shabby knapsack on his shoulder and gave him a gnarled stick. Nobody would ever recognize in this repulsive old man the great Odysseus who had at last returned to Ithaca!

Athene transformed Odysseus into an old man.

119

BOOK XIV

So walking with difficulty Odysseus moved along the rocky paths of his beloved island, up towards the forests that crowned the tall mountain. From the crest of a hill he saw, there amongst the oak trees and olive trees, Eumaeus' hut and the wide pen where he kept the sows and boars. Every day with a heavy sigh, faithful Eumaeus had to pick the fattest animal and send it to the palace for the Suitors' banquet.

There was Eumaeus, sitting with a sombre face, making a pair of leather sandals for himself. Suddenly he heard the dogs bark fiercely. He raised his eyes and saw a strange old man surrounded by the barking animals. 'Down, down!' shouted Eumaeus, rising at once from his seat. And as the dogs moved away a little, he said, 'Old man, you narrowly escaped being torn to pieces by my dogs! Come, come inside, let us drink a cup of wine. Then you can tell me who you are.'

'Thank you my friend. The gods love a man who welcomes strangers as you do. Especially when strangers are as old as I am.'

'Quite. You speak well. It is a sin to reject a visitor!' Eumaeus scattered some brushwood on the floor, covered it with the skin of a wild goat and said, 'Sit here, and make yourself comfortable! You are hungry old man, I can see it, and you are weak. Then we shall eat together.'

'I thank you for greeting me so heartily.'

'Yes, old man, but there is another I should also like to welcome . . .' Eumaeus said with a sigh. 'Had he come back I would not be here, fearing!'

'Fear? You are frightened? Why?'

'Because on this island, my king no longer rules. Instead the rulers are a gang of arrogant young men who have taken over. And as you see, I am forced to work for them. If my king were here, everything would be different . . . Well, he won't come though. Too much time has passed. He must have died by now, on some distant land or in some shipwreck. . . . But wait, I shall find something to eat.'

They both began to eat and Odysseus asked cautiously, 'Friend, you spoke of your king of

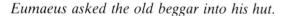

Eumaeus asked the old beggar into his hut.

whom nobody knows anything. Tell me his name. I have travelled much, I have seen many places, heard many tales. Who knows, I may have news for you.'

Eumaeus shook his head. 'All foreigners who come to Ithaca speak like you. All think they know. Many go to my lady, Queen Penelope, and she, poor soul, hears them all and their words keep her hopes alive. No, old man, it is useless to deceive oneself. Odysseus — for that is the name of my king — must by now be dead. Never more, even if I were to circle the world, would I find another master like him! He loved me you know! It might seem strange to you that a king could love a herdsman. But to Odysseus nothing was strange!'

For a while both ate in silence. Eumaeus was moved and troubled. Odysseus noticed this and told him softly, 'Why shouldn't he come back? You must have faith.'

'I have no more faith.'

'And what if he did come back? If, in some way or other Odysseus did return to Ithaca? . . .'

'In that case . . . but no, no. It is impossible.'

'Listen, my friend, I tell you seriously — it is not idle talk — I tell you as a solemn promise, that Odysseus will return!'

'They are just words!'

'No. Odysseus will come back. He will return, he will go back to his home and will punish all those who offend and dishonour his wife and son! Would you be prepared to give me a new mantle and tunic if my words were to come true?'

Eumaeus smiled bitterly. 'Yes, I shall give you a new tunic and mantle. But, my friend, I shall never give them to you because I know all too well that my king will never see Ithaca again. Now drink stranger, and let us talk about something else. When I talk about these things, about my master, I feel a heaviness in my heart and everything seems ugly and pointless.'

'And what about your king's son . . .'

Eumaeus poured wine for his guest.

'Telemachus? He is a very good young man, very brave. But what can he do, tell me, against the Suitors? He is strong but he never had a father to teach him about arms in battle. If they wanted to, the Suitors could kill him anytime . . . Not now though. He went to Sparta to find out news of Odysseus. He was wrong to go, he should not have left his mother alone! And in my opinion he must have lost his mind to go to sea after what happened to his father.' A long silence followed in which only the distant echo of the waves could be heard, relentlessly crashing against the rocky coastline. Then Eumaeus said again, 'But tell me about yourself, old man. You are not from here — I have never seen you. Who are you? Where do you come from? You say that you have travelled much, and it must be true for I see that your strength has gone with your mouth. Tell me then. If we talk about you we won't talk about Odysseus anymore. I cannot bear what is happening on this island!'

Odysseus drank and replied, 'My friend, you

Eumaeus slept with the pigs to keep watch over them.

want to know my story . . . Well, even if I spoke for hours and hours, it would not be sufficient to tell you all. I shall only tell you now that I was rich and powerful once and that I have fought under the walls of Troy. There I met Odysseus. And I also heard from Pheidon, king of the Thesprotian, where I arrived after a thousand adventures. Pheidon told me that shortly before my arrival Odysseus had been in his palace. The king told me that he welcomed him and gave him hospitality on his homeward journey.'

'But . . . then? Why hasn't he returned?' asked Eumaeus.

'I don't know. From Pheidon's palace, Odysseus left to consult an oracle. I know no more.'

'If my master went to consult an oracle, if he escaped death under Troy, it means that there is still hope! . . . ' Eumaeus exclaimed. 'But no,' he then added, shaking his head, 'no. Too late. If Odysseus has not yet reached home it means he never will.'

'I see that nothing can convince you. All right. We have agreed then, if your master comes back, you will give me a mantle and a tunic!'

Eumaeus stood up and answered almost absent-mindedly, 'So be it! I shall give you those things if my master returns!'

'What are you looking at?' asked Odysseus.

'Ah, here they come,' was the answer. 'Some friends were to eat with me and here they are now!'

Indeed, more herdsmen were returning from their day's work and Eumaeus went to them. 'Friends, we have a guest, who has travelled much. Bring the fattest pig. Just for once the Suitors will not have the fattest for themselves!' The pig was slaughtered, skinned and roasted on the spit. Eumaeus carefully carved it and the rustic banquet began. Odysseus said, 'Thank you, O Eumaeus! You honour me with the best pieces!'

'Eat, stranger, and drink some more. Let us all drink friends,' added Eumaeus with a sad face, 'to the one who is far away and yet remains always in our hearts. Let us drink to our king Odysseus!'

So they ate and drank, and as they did so the shadows of night fell rapidly. The sky clouded over and it started to rain. As the rain fell outside, Odysseus began talking again. 'Hear, my friends, what happened when many years ago I was fighting under Troy. I went with Menelaus and Odysseus to lay an ambush on a Trojan patrol. We waited for many hours in the bushes and an icy rain started to fall. I had not brought my cloak and I was frozen to the bone. Shivering, I told Odysseus. In order to help me, he whispered, "I need a volunteer to run to camp and find out whether someone will come to our help at the time of battle!" A soldier rose at once and ran off leaving his cloak behind. Odysseus then handed it over to me saying, "Here! Don't die of cold, cover yourself!" '

Hearing this tale, all praised Odysseus' cunning and Eumaeus said, 'Very well old man, you can be sure that you will not die of cold tonight either!' And when his guests had gone home he added leaves to the bed, inviting Odysseus to stretch out on it, and covered him with his worn out mantle.

Eumaeus did not sleep in the hut. Even if his master was dead, as he thought, he must guard his pigs. He took a sword and went to settle down outside in a small cave sheltered from the wind. Odysseus, with his eyes half shut, whispered, 'You shall have your reward faithful Eumaeus!'

BOOK XV

Athene, meanwhile, had reached Sparta. Invisible in Menelaus' stately palace, she approached Telemachus who slept restlessly, anxious as he was about his father. She whispered softly in his ear, 'What are you doing still here, Telemachus? It is wrong of you to linger abroad and leave your house in the hands of a bunch of scoundrels who are intent on wasting your father's wealth and on taking your mother away from you.' In his sleep the youth moaned softly and Athene went on, 'If then, pressed by her parents, Penelope married Eurymachus, the handsomest and strongest of the Suitors, what will happen to your own possessions if you are not at home? Go. Take leave of Menelaus and go at once, for your place is in Ithaca. But beware and keep away as far as possible from the straits between the islands of Ithaca and Samos, for a ship is waiting to ambush you. Do not even stop at night. As soon as you have reached Ithaca, run to the swineherd Eumaeus who looks after your pigs.'

Having spoken thus, the goddess kept quiet. Telemachus awoke, stood up and looked at the sky eager for the new day to dawn. In fact, he now understood that he had stayed away too long. No sooner had the sun risen than he presented himself to Menelaus to ask his permission to leave. Menelaus heard him, understood and said, 'Yes, it is right that you should go, Telemachus. Leave then and may your journey be a safe one.'

After taking leave of the beautiful Helen, Telemachus returned to Pylos and boarded his ship where his companions eagerly waited for him. With loosened sails the swift vessel forged ahead towards Ithaca.

As Telemachus sailed, Eumaeus in his hut was getting ready for a day's work. He had something to eat with his helpers. Odysseus, still in the disguise of an old beggar, sat with them and, drinking some soup, he asked, 'Tell me Eumaeus, does Odysseus still have a father? And a mother?'

Telemachus' ship returned to Ithaca.

Odysseus asked Eumaeus for news of his father.

'Certainly, he still has his father. He is Laertes, the kindest and most unfortunate man I have ever met. You see, stranger, until Odysseus left home, Laertes lived in the palace. Of course he was too old to fight, to tame horses, to lead ships, but he could still hunt. Now, poor soul, he lives in a hut like this one, and every day he weeps over the death of his son . . . As for his mother, well she died of heartache, longing for her son. All is lost. Laertes is a peasant, Penelope is detained by the Suitors, and Telemachus is too young to fight them. You see there are many sad happenings on the island of Ithaca.'

'Yes, I understand. But tell me, Eumaeus, suppose I went to the palace and offered my services to the Suitors?'

'What! Are you mad, old man?'

'No. I mean to say that I cannot stay here with you. It is right that I should earn my daily bread. Oh yes I could always beg, but I don't like it. I prefer working. No-one can chop wood with such accuracy, no-one can build a fire as well as I can, and what is more, I can do other thngs like carve meat, look after wine . . . I am a good cook and an excellent cup-bearer . . .'

Eumaeus raised his hands so as to prevent him from saying any more. 'Enough, stranger. Speak no more. If you must go to the palace, first hear what I have to tell you. Do you want to court death? The Suitors are impudent, pitiless scoundrels, and their servants are just the same. They are all smartly dressed, all perfumed with their hair well greased in oil. If you present yourself there you will only suffer abuse and humiliation! No, stay with me. You are not a nuisance to anyone.'

'But,' Odysseus went on, weighing Eumaeus' honesty and loyalty, 'if I stay I shall be eating Telemachus' food.'

'Indeed. And since Telemachus will soon be back he will be the one to decide whether you can stay or not. I think,' Eumaeus said with the approval of the other swineherds, 'that he will ask you to stay and provide you with a tunic and a cloak, and that he will see that you reach your destination, wherever that may be.'

'Let us hope that Telemachus shall return soon then,' murmured Odysseus.

Telemachus meanwhile was sailing towards home. Faithful to the orders given by the mysterious voice, he steered a course well away from the islands that dotted the shimmering Greek seas — large ones, small ones, some mere barren rocks. Not even at night did he give the order to lower the sails. He stood by the helmsman who, with his eyes peering at the stars, guided the ship towards Ithaca. The Suitors, waiting in the straits of Samos, noticed nothing. It was dawn when the ship reached its mooring.

'Go ashore my friends,' said Telemachus to his companions. 'I will join you presently.'

Telemachus arrived at Eumaeus' hut.

'Must we tell your mother of your arrival?' asked one of the sailors, Theoclymenus.

'Not yet. Anyhow it is not easy to see her. She stays alone in her rooms, weaving all day long. Don't tell her anything.'

'Look!' someone shouted at that moment. All looked up. Directly above the ship a falcon had appeared clutching in its talons a dove whose feathers had been torn away by the bird of prey and were falling on to the ship. It happened within seconds and with a great shriek the falcon flew away again. Somebody whispered, 'This is an omen sent by the gods, Telemachus. Something is about to happen in our land.'

'What is to happen will happen', Telemachus answered sternly. Then taking his spear he said, 'It is agreed then. Go to the city. We shall meet later.'

With that he took the road to the mountains and walked to Eumaeus' hut. He had strange thoughts in his mind. 'Yes, probably the apparition of the falcon was an omen . . . but what did it mean? What was the significance of the bird of prey with the dove savagely plucked and destined to die? . . . Will someone die in Ithaca soon? But who? Perhaps he himself, Telemachus? . . . Yes, perhaps. Most certainly!' thought the youth as he walked with great strides along the paths amongst the olive trees, the rocks, and the green fields. 'In fact I stand alone against all the Suitors. And if they did not succeed in reaching me at sea they can do it whenever they choose to in the palace. If they want to they can kill me even in my rooms. And who will then bring comfort to my mother?'

Telemachus tried to keep these gloomy thoughts away until he came in sight of Eumaeus' hut. The swineherd's dogs, which had scented someone approaching, leapt up snapping and snarling. When they saw Telemachus though, they ran to him wagging their tails in a friendly way. They knew this young man well — he was their friend and their master's friend. They leapt on him to be patted and scratched, and so Telemachus, surrounded by dogs, drew near the hut.

'Eumaeus!' he called out. 'Eumaeus! Are you there? . . .'

BOOK XVI

Inside the hut, Odysseus said to Eumaeus, 'My friend, you have a visitor who is familiar to your dogs for they do not bark. On the contrary, from what I can see from here they are giving him a warm welcome.'

'Who could it be?' whispered Eumaeus. And there on the threshold appeared Telemachus. Eumaeus, upon seeing him leapt to his feet dropping a full jug of wine. He stretched out his arms and bit his lips in an effort to suppress his tears of joy, but he could not hold them back and they streamed down his face. 'You are here, Telemachus, light of my days,' he exclaimed in a broken voice. 'I . . . yes I feared I would not see you again, my dear boy! I feared that . . . Oh! Let me embrace you Telemachus, if you will!' Throwing his arms around the faithful old man, Telemachus said, 'Eumaeus, I am alive as you see. And I come to you to hear what has happened while I was away. How is my mother? . . .' and he added, 'Is she still my mother or has she remarried?'

'Oh no!' answered the swineherd at once. 'No, she resists! She weeps but she resists!'

'I understand,' whispered Telemachus, and at that moment he noticed Odysseus who was looking at him intensely from under the worn hood. He rose as if to give him his seat. 'No,

stranger, keep your seat,' he said. 'Eumaeus will find me another, won't you Eumaeus?'

'Here, on these sweet smelling leaves my dear boy! Sit here!' As he sat down and set his spear against the wall, Telemachus asked, 'Where do you come from old man? I don't think I have seen you on Ithaca before. And who brought you here? You certainly did not come on foot.'

'He comes from Crete,' answered Eumaeus, 'and he has been round the world! I have kept him here with me, Telemachus, but now I entrust him to you for you are the lord in Ithaca!'

Telemachus smiled bitterly. 'I? No, the lords are the Suitors who live in the palace, who eat and drink off me, who squander my wealth . . . and who will perhaps kill me soon. But never mind. Stay here if you wish, old man, I will send you clothes and food. I should like you to be my guest at the palace but I am not the master in my father's house any more.'

'Eumaeus told me your father's story,' murmured Odysseus, 'and I am sure that he will come back.'

'May it be the gods' will. Eumaeus,' Telemachus said, 'please go to the city, to my mother, and tell her I am here. I shall go to her tonight when the Suitors are asleep.'

Eumaeus rose. 'I shall obey you, Telemachus!' he said humbly, and set off. And there outside the hut appeared Athene. Neither Telemachus nor the swineherd saw her. But the dogs could see her and they ran away whimpering. Odysseus could also see her so at once he came out of the hut to greet her. 'Odysseus', the goddess said to him, 'speak to your son immediately. Let him in on your secret and plot your revenge with him!'

With these words Athene tapped Odysseus with her wand and he instantly resumed his own appearance. Again he became tall, broad-shouldered and vigorous, with his proud face and bright, intelligent eyes. While Athene disappeared, Odysseus went back into the hut.

Eumaeus greeted Telemachus.

Upon seeing him Telemachus stood up in amazement. 'You are certainly different from the man who just went out, stranger . . .' he stuttered. 'Are you a god? If you are, have mercy upon us!'

'No! I am not a god, Telemachus,' replied Odysseus. 'I am your father!'

'My father!' exclaimed the youth, growing pale. 'But . . . but how is it possible? . . . Just a minute ago . . .'

'Just a minute ago I was a poor old man, yes. And now by the will of Athene I am myself again. My son Telemachus,' and Odysseus opened his mighty arms, 'here I am back home after twenty years!'

Weeping with joy, Telemachus threw himself into his father's arms. Odysseus held him for a long time, mingling his own tears with those of his son. Finally he said, 'Listen, Telemachus, we must act and act very fast. Tell me, how many Suitors are there? Can we take them on, the two of us, or are they too many?'

Athene tapped Odysseus with her wand and he resumed his true appearance.

Weeping with joy, Telemachus embraced his father.

'The two of us alone? Oh, no father! Counting their servants they are about one hundred. We need allies or we shall not succeed!'

'Allies indeed!' Odysseus said calmly. 'We shall have two.'

'Only two?'

'Yes, Athene and Zeus. With them, my son, victory is ours. Listen to me now. Go to the palace. Be gentle and humble with the Suitors so that they do not harm you . . . I shall come too, but under the disguise of the old beggar. Don't worry if they hurt me, rather try to get hold of the weapons hanging on the walls of the hall and take them where they won't be found.'

'But how?' asked the confused Telemachus. Odysseus was prompt to answer. 'Tell them that next to the fire, the weapons will be tarnished, or that you want to avoid a brawl. Have ready for us two spears, two swords and two shields . . . The gods will think of the rest. Go! Ah, one more thing. Do not tell a soul that I have returned, neither my father, nor

Odysseus was again turned into an old beggar by Athene.

Eumaeus nor your mother Penelope! Do you swear it?'

'I shall carry out your orders, father,' Telemachus answered and, his heart beating wildly, he hastened down towards the city and the palace.

In the meantime, Athene appeared to Odysseus. 'Yes,' she told him, 'I shall be at your side during the struggle. In the meanwhile go back to your old beggar disguise!' A wave of her hand and the transformation was completed.

While all this had happened up in the hills, in the palace the Suitors were talking about Telemachus' return. They had seen his ship in the harbour. 'So he has avoided the ambush. He is still here, that snivelling brat!'

'It is better this way! Some things are better done on land than at sea. We shall wait for the right time and then we shall get rid of him! One thing is certain, young Telemachus will not live a long life!' A roar of laughter greeted these words. And the Suitors resumed their games and their feasting, and did not even notice Telemachus walking through the resplendent hall of the palace and going up the stairs to the rooms of the beautiful and wise Penelope.

She greeted him with tearful eyes. 'My son, light of my life, you are back! What have you learnt? I was so frightened for you! Eumaeus the swineherd was here a little while ago and told me the news of your arrival! Tell me, what did you hear while you were in Sparta?'

'Nothing of my father,' Telemachus said, lowering his eyes. 'Unfortunately nothing. I spoke to Menelaus, to the divine Helen . . . Nothing. Mother,' he added, 'in spite of all, we must wait a few days more. Wait and give no answer to these impudent villains who have settled down in this house and that I . . . I . . .'

'Calm yourself, my son. I will not cease to hope and to wait. No, we won't tell them anything, although their insistence is unbearable. I will stay here and I will do whatever you tell me to do. But you,' added Penelope embracing her son, 'you must be very careful! They want to kill you, you know!'

'Perhaps they will die before me!' answered Telemachus calmly. Then the two of them went to confront the Suitors. Penelope angrily accused them of despoiling the house of Odysseus, a man to whom many owed their lives and plotting to dishonour his family. Her outburst left them silent and sullen.

Meanwhile Odysseus, who was an old beggar once again, was talking with Eumaeus who had returned to his hut. 'I want to go down to the city, Eumaeus,' he said, 'to the palace to beg. You know . . . I am too old to work.'

'As you wish. Come, I shall accompany you . . . but beware! If you go into the palace I fear the Suitors will not treat you well! . . . Let us away!'

BOOK XVII

They both left and soon reached the gardens behind the palace. There on a dung heap lay a sick, old dog full of ticks, who suddenly raised his head, pricked up his ears, looked at Odysseus with liquid eyes and wagged his tail. Odysseus could hardly contain his emotion and brushed a tear away. Argus! This was his faithful dog Argus! . . . The dog had recognized him. In a broken voice he stuttered, 'Eumaeus . . . that dog . . .'

'Yes, he was Odysseus' dog, look at him, poor thing. No-one looks after him! . . .' Odysseus would have liked to pat poor Argus, but he would have betrayed himself. So he went on into the palace . . . and Argus died. His weak, faithful heart could not withstand the emotion of seeing his beloved master again.

Odysseus went into the great hall where the Suitors were assembled around a banquet. Clothed in filthy rags and walking with the help of a stick, Odysseus humbly sat down on the step just by the door. Telemachus saw him, called Eumaeus and gave him a whole loaf of bread. 'Take it to the old man,' he said, 'and tell him to beg from each man in turn. Begging is not shameful when one is so poor.' Odysseus took the bread and ate it slowly. Then as Eumaeus had suggested, he stood up and started to go from one suitor to the other, stretching out his old hand to beg.

Bewildered, the Suitors wondered who this bedraggled old man was. 'It is not known who he is,' said one of the servants. 'Eumaeus the swineherd brought him.'

'Ha, indeed!' exclaimed Antinous. 'A fine gift you have brought Eumaeus. You keep saying that we eat too much and yet you bring a guest to our table!' At these words, the Suitors laughed and Eumaeus proudly replied, 'Antinous, as long as Penelope lives in this palace, and Telemachus with her, I shall invite the poor on their behalf!'

'Be quiet, Eumaeus,' Telemachus intervened. 'Do not speak so, do not irritate Antinous! . . .' But it was too late. Antinous was already red in the face!

Argus the dog recognized his master.

'Ha!' he exclaimed. 'So this is what you think? Well, look Eumaeus, if we all gave that filthy old man what I will give him, he would not come here to bother us for at least three months!' And so saying he picked up a foot stool and showed it to everybody, adding 'Here, this will be my gift!'

Odysseus controlled himself, although his blood was boiling in his veins, and remaining humble, continued round the assembly holding out his hand. Many amongst the Suitors gave him bread and meat and indeed very good pieces. At last he came round to Antinous. 'My lord,' Odysseus said, 'you seem the noblest among your friends. You must therefore give me the best piece of all. I too, you know, once had a rich palace and I too . . .' Antinous, infuriated, interrupted him. 'Enough! What do I care about the story of your life, you old ragbag! Stop where you are! Don't come near me!'

Odysseus stopped, and turning away he said,

'Very well, I shall go. I thought you a noble man but you are not since you will not even give me a piece of bread!' Antinous heard him and in a fury he picked up the stool and flung it at Odysseus, striking him full on the right shoulder. Such was the violence of the blow and the weight of the stool that any man would have fallen under such an impact. But Odysseus did not fall. He stood firm on his feet and in the great silence he said, 'Antinous, fate will punish you for what you have done!' Then he went to a corner of the room and, pale in the face, he started to eat what the Suitors had given him. Impressed, the Suitors whispered amongst themselves. 'Really, Antinous was wrong to strike the old man! He could be a god in disguise, who knows? . . .'

The banquet went on and so did the talking and laughing. Suddenly in the great hall appeared Irus, a notorious vagabond who always looked hungry and thirsty. He was also notorious for his stupidity. He was a large man but without real strength or dignity and he

Antinous threw a heavy stool at Odysseus.

assumed an air of arrogant haughtiness. The Suitors always made fun of him behind his back. And it was indeed to please the Suitors that he now moved forward and turned to Odysseus saying, 'Hey! What are you doing here ugly old man? Clear off, understand? Or I'll take you by your ankle and drag you out myself!' Odysseus replied, 'Irus, we are both poor. Why do you insult me? Eat and drink as I do without provoking me, if you wish to ever set foot in this palace again!'

'Listen to the wretched man's talk! Well perhaps you want to fight me? But mind, I am younger than you and I can really give you a good thrashing and drag you out by your ankle!'

Odysseus rose and Antinous exclaimed, 'Friends, if these two beggars fight, we shall indeed witness an interesting spectacle. Listen, the winner shall be entitled to come and eat our leftovers every day and he will be the only beggar allowed in. What do you say?'

BOOK XVIII

The Suitors approved with cries of joy. And Irus, preparing for the fight shouted, 'I'll smash all his teeth in! Come on then ragamuffin, if you've got the nerve!' So saying he struck a blow on Odysseus' right shoulder . . . in a split second Odysseus retorted with a punch of his mighty fist, hitting Irus under his eye. There was the chilling noise of crushed bones. Irus fell on his face vomiting blood. There was a great hush. All the Suitors watched in utter amazement. Then Odysseus grabbed Irus by the ankle and dragged him outside, rolling him in the dust. 'There! and now stay outside Irus,' he said, sitting him up against the wall, 'and keep the dogs and pigs away!'

Odysseus went back into the palace where the Suitors were whispering in bewilderment. They felt a mixture of anger, admiration and spite. 'Who can he be?' mumbled someone, 'this beggar so quick with words and fists?' Odysseus did not look around him, but went back to his corner, sat down and continued eating. Some of the Suitors were about to speak to him, provoke him, perhaps to insult him, when in the door, beautiful and solemn, Penelope appeared.

Everyone fell silent. Everyone looked at her. And she, made even more splendid than ever through Athene's divine spell, seemed to be the woman most worthy of love. Everyone hoped that her gaze would rest upon him. But Penelope turned to Telemachus and said sternly, 'I was told, my son, that this man, this stranger, was insulted and persecuted. It is very sad that such a thing can happen under Odysseus' roof. Any stranger is sacred, poor or wealthy, prince or pauper.'

'Mother,' answered Telemachus, 'I can do nothing against these people who sit at our table!'

Then Eurymachus rose and exclaimed, 'Penelope, we know we annoy you because there are too many of us in your house! But you see,' he added, 'you are so beautiful that it is a

Odysseus grabbed Irus by the ankle and dragged him outside.

wonder we should be so few!' Someone laughed, but Penelope retorted, 'No, you annoy me because most of all you are greedy and petty men. You intend to marry me and yet you eat and drink my wealth away, you claim to love me and yet you insult me in this very house. If my husband Odysseus were here, which one amongst you would have the audacity to behave as he does?' There was no answer.

And Odysseus, sitting in his corner, felt comforted in his heart. Yes, his dear wife, the sight of whom had sent a shiver through his body, had not forgotten him. She still loved him and despised all the Suitors who wanted to marry her. Yes, it was worth suffering for a woman such as Penelope. Meanwhile the Suitors, stung by the Queen's words competed against one another by bestowing gifts upon her. Penelope gave them all an icy stare and returned to her rooms.

Night had fallen. This had been a day unlike any other day because the vagrant stranger had come and brought trouble. But in fact it had been a day like any other because the Suitors ate and drank from the wealth of the man whom they thought by now lost and whom they were sure would never return.

Great fires were lit. Odysseus went from one to the other poking them and stirring them up. Eurymachus said, 'Friends, look! I truly believe the man has been sent from heaven. He hasn't a hair on his head and his bald crown shines bright!' Amongst the roars of laughter, he went on, 'Hey, stranger, what do you say? Would you like to work for me? You would be well paid. Or would you rather stay here and beg for your food? Come on, answer me old ragbag!'

'Eurymachus,' answered Odysseus after a pause, 'if we were at war, both armed, perhaps you would not talk to me like this. You insult me because you feel safe amongst your friends. But if Odysseus were here then that wide door

In the door appeared the beautiful and solemn Penelope.

there would seem too narrow, so great would be your hurry to escape!'

Growing livid with anger at these words, Eurymachus grabbed a stool and, as a while earlier Antinous had done, he threw it at Odysseus. It missed him but instead hit the cup-bearer of Amphimonus, another young noble, and severed the man's hand and he fell to the ground unconscious. There was great turmoil. One of the Suitors shouted, 'Enough! Have you taken leave of your senses, quarreling over some insignificant vagrant?'

'Yes, you've gone mad,' exclaimed Telemachus. 'You are drunk. You had better go and sleep it off!'

'Quite so!' replied one of the Suitors after a moment's silence. 'Telemachus is right. Perhaps we have drunk too much. So then, one last cup of wine, my friends and let each go and sleep where he chooses!' So it was that in the red glow of the fires, the Suitors drank one more time and then left in their chariots. At last silence fell on the palace.

No sooner had the last chariot disappeared at the end of the courtyard than Odysseus turned to Telemachus. 'Quick, my son,' he said pointing at a huge array of spears, swords, shields and helmets hanging on the wall over the large fireplace, 'let us remove these weapons from the wall and stow them away where the Suitors will not find them! There is no time to lose! Send the maids away. We shall take care of everything . . . If the Suitors ask where you have put the arms you will answer that you have sent them to be polished as the smoke had tarnished them!' Telemachus promptly obeyed, and working quickly and silently they carried the arms into a secret chamber of the palace, where nobody would find them.

'And now leave, Telemachus,' Odysseus said. 'I hear your mother coming down. Go. I wish to speak to her alone.'

The Suitors left the palace on their chariots.

BOOK XIX

The young man left and soon after, followed by her maids, Penelope arrived. She sat at the loom and began to weave in silence. Odysseus had bowed deeply when he saw her, and after a while she said, 'Stranger, come nearer!'

'Here I am Madam,' he answered, kneeling to the ground.

'Who are you? Where do you come from?'

'Does it matter to you who I am? I come from the distant Isle of Crete. I was rich and powerful once until Zeus struck me.'

'I understand. He struck me too, taking away my husband whom I loved so much and whom I still love. Did you see how the Suitors are getting more arrogant by the day. They demand that I make up my mind and marry one of them. I have stood firm for ten years, but I cannot resist any longer. In a few days, with a heavy heart I shall have to make a choice.'

'But,' whispered Odysseus, 'what if your husband did return?'

'He will not. Alas! He will not any more. And I shall be condemned to an unhappy life. You see, for four years I was able to deceive the Suitors with a simple trick. I wove a cloth — it will be a shroud, I said, for Laertes, my husband's father. When I have finished it I shall choose one of you and I shall become his wife. Well, stranger, I wove by day, and by night I unthreaded my work so that it seemed my work was endless. But one of my maids,' she went on bitterly, 'revealed my secret. I have been found out. Since then I have done nothing but defend myself . . . Now I am too tired.'

'Woman, you are faithful to Odysseus, I can see it. Well then, I shall disclose something to you which I have never told anyone . . .'

'What are you talking about?' asked Penelope anxiously.

'I have seen your husband in Crete.'

'You lie!'

'No. He wore a red cloak with an embossed brooch with a hound clutching a fawn in its teeth.'

Odysseus spoke to Penelope.

Whilst washing Odysseus' feet, Eurycleia discovered an old scar and recognized him.

'Yes,' said Penelope shaking with emotion and unable to withold her tears, 'I gave him that cloak and brooch.'

'Do not weep, for I know — and do not ask me how — that Odysseus is about to return. He has travelled much, he has seen many places, and overcome many dangers. He has lost all his dearest friends, his entire fleet, but he is safe. And he will be back, and sooner than you think!'

'Old man, may Zeus hear you,' whispered Penelope. 'Alas, I don't believe in it any more. I have hoped for too long, I have deceived myself with illusions in order to keep my faith alive. In any case, from now on you shall be an honoured guest in this house for you have made my heart beat with renewed hope, even if it is soon to faint away. Maids!' she called out, 'wash this man's feet and prepare him a comfortable bed. He will sit at the table with the others and Heaven help anyone who dares to insult him!'

Odysseus was moved by these words, but he controlled himself, and still on his knees he answered, 'Woman faithful to Odysseus, son of Laertes, I do not want to sleep in a comfortable bed. I would rather lie on the barren earth. Nor do I want your maids to wash my feet. They are all too young for me and some have insulted and scorned me because young girls dislike old people like me. But,' he added, 'if you have an old servant who has suffered and understands grief, then yes, I should gladly accept having my feet washed.'

Penelope smiled sadly. 'You are wise, stranger. There is indeed such an old servant, wise and kind-hearted. This woman looked after Odysseus from the day he was born. Eurycleia is her name. She is weary and worn out because time passes and leaves it mark. She will wash your feet.' She then turned and said, 'Eurycleia, come and wash the feet of a man who bears news of your lord and master, my beloved Odysseus.'

Eurycleia came at once, her eyes red with weeping. 'Ah, my lord, Zeus has not been kind to you,' she said, 'for he has struck you and forced you to wander as a beggar from land to land. Yes, I shall wash your feet. Perhaps', she added crying, 'the same fate has befallen my king and master Odysseus. Give me your feet. I shall wash you.'

Thereupon Odysseus withdrew some distance from Penelope and sat on a stool. Penelope had resumed her work, and old Eurycleia fetched a basin of warm water. Kneeling down in front of him and before starting to wash his feet, she whispered to him, 'Ah, stranger, of all the people who have come here . . . I have never seen anyone who looked so much like Odysseus!'

'Old people all look the same, you know!'

'Give me your leg. Perhaps you are right!' Odysseus stretched out his leg towards Eurycleia who had begun to wash it. But suddenly

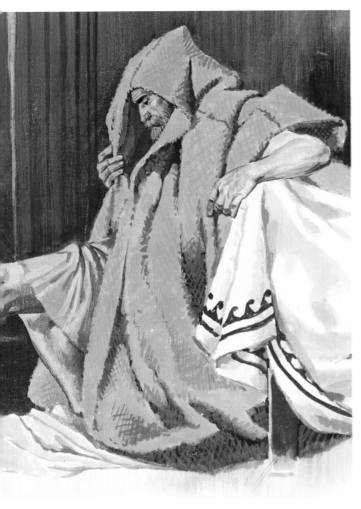

the hero remembered a scar he had on that very leg, left by a wound from the tusk of a wild boar, received many, many years ago during a hunting party. Eurycleia knew the scar well for she had washed his legs time and time again. 'What if she recognizes it,' thought Odysseus, 'and starts screaming, revealing my identity? . . .'

He was about to get up. But too late! Washing his leg, Eurycleia had seen the scar and she touched it with trembling hands. She had recognized it. Shaking and breathless she dropped Odysseus' foot in the basin and the water splashed on the ground. Overcome with joy, Eurycleia tried to shout, 'Odysseus, you are back!' but in her excitement was only able to mumble some garbled words. She turned to Penelope and was about to announce that Odysseus had come back, when he put his hand over her mouth and whispered, 'Eurycleia, do you wish to ruin me? You have fed me as a child, do you want to kill me now?'

She listened to him with wide eyes and nobody noticed what had happened, for Athene had distracted Penelope's attention as well as that of her maids', by casting a spell on them. 'My child,' stuttered Eurycleia as soon as Odysseus had released her, 'fear not and trust me!'

'Be faithful!' warned Odysseus again. Eurycleia continued to wash his feet. She had just finished drying and annointing them with perfumed oil when Penelope came over to them. 'Stranger,' she said, 'I have been thinking. I must make up my mind and I shall do it tomorrow. I shall have the twelve great axes belonging to my husband lined up in the ground. Each one has a ring on its head. Odysseus could shoot an arrow straight through them all. This will be my proposal to the Suitors: I shall marry the one who can shoot an arrow through the ring of all twelve axes using Odysseus' bow!'

Odysseus understood. Penelope hoped that none of her suitors would succeed in the challenge. 'Yes, honoured lady,' he said, 'it is a very good idea. You will see that before the Suitors can even draw the bow your husband Odysseus will have returned.'

'May the gods hear you!' Penelope whispered, her heart greatly perturbed, and followed by her maids she left. 'Why does the old man speak so? Is he truly inspired by the gods to say such words? Is it possible that Odysseus will return tomorrow at last, and save me? . . .' she wondered.

Lying down on deer skin, Odysseus tried to get to sleep in the great hall of the palace. But he could not. He heard the voices of the maids, who, as soon as Penelope had left, went out and joined the Suitors. Revenge would also be carried out on them, thought the hero, so that his house would be cleansed of all treason. He would have mercy on no-one. Penelope had suffered too much.

BOOK XX

As he tried to sleep, Odysseus could only think of his faithful wife's eyes, reddened by so many tears. Anger shook him . . . He could hardly contain himself. But he had to keep calm, he had to control himself, for tomorrow he would have to fight hard, alone against the Suitors . . . Never mind. He would win . . .

But sleep still did not come. Then Athene appeared to him and whispered, 'Do not fret, Odysseus. Do not fear. You are alone against a hundred, but I am at your side. Sleep now. You will need all your strength tomorrow.'

Odysseus wanted to talk to her, ask her questions, but Athene lulled him to sleep and soon he was dead to the world.

The maids began preparing for the feast.

The next morning he was woken up by the voices of the maids. They were already preparing the hall for the big banquet. By then it was known that Penelope had decided to remarry and would choose her future husband. Therefore the palace had to sparkle and the fattest cows had to be slaughtered and the pitchers filled with the sweetest wine. Already a messenger had been sent to the mountains to have Eumaeus bring the fattest pigs and sheep. Already the paving stones, the marble floors, the golden friezes were being scrubbed. The good smell of freshly baked bread filled the air. Odysseus could smell it and thought, 'That's right, let the Suitors sit at the banquet, it shall be their last meal!'

Precious rugs were spread out, and by the huge fireplaces, piles of fragrant wood were brought.

Telemachus had also risen and immediately asked news of the stranger. 'He ate and drank very little, my child,' Eurycleia told him 'and he talked to your mother for a very long time.'

'Where is he now?'

'In the hall, my child.'

Odysseus had gone out into the hallway and there, between the splendid columns, he saw Eumaeus, the good and obedient swineherd, who had brought the pigs down to the city with an assistant. 'Stranger, have the Suitors insulted you again?' he asked clasping Odysseus' hands.

'Whoever insults the guests in someone else's house will be harshly punished by the gods, Eumaeus!'

'Let us hope it shall be so. Look, more animals for these impudent devils! But tell me, is it true what they say, that today the wise Penelope is to choose her future husband?'

'There is no telling what will happen today,' answered Odysseus.

And suddenly a clamour was heard, of pawing horses and loud voices. The Suitors had arrived and entered the palace. Outside the slaughter of the cattle had begun. The roasting spits were being prepared. Telemachus, who had found Odysseus at last, said to him in a loud voice, 'You will sit next to me, stranger. And

In the palace hall, Odysseus met Eumaeus.

nobody will dare insult you!' Food and wine were finally served. One by one the Suitors took their seats at the table, and one of them — Ctesippus — who had heard Telemachus, exclaimed, 'You are quite right young man! That old ragged man must sit at the table with us! It is only fair that he should have his share! Look, I shall give him a tasty morsel right away, and may he enjoy it!' With this he hurled a leg of beef at Odysseus, who barely had time to duck his head.

Telemachus leapt to his feet. 'Better for you Ctesippus, that you missed, otherwise I would have taken revenge for the offence done to me in this way!' And he showed his spear. Someone shouted then, 'Enough! We have not come here to quarrel like yesterday!'

'Hear, hear! Enough of this squabbling!'

'Ever since the arrival of the stranger we have done nothing but quarrel!' The banquet continued in reasonable order. Suddenly the Suitors dropped their conversation. There on the threshold, Penelope appeared, followed by her train of maids. In her hand she held a mighty bow and a quiver full of arrows.

In the silence which fell upon the assembly, she turned her sparkling eyes to the men sitting at the banquet table and said, 'Listen to me, all of you who have lived in this house for far too long with the excuse that you wished to marry me. Listen. I have made a decision. I shall put your strength and skill to the test with this bow that belongs to my unforgettable husband. My maids,' she pointed at the girls, 'are carrying twelve axes, each of which has a ring on it. I promise to marry the one amongst you who can shoot an arrow through all twelve rings. Eumaeus, here is the bow, show it to the Suitors.'

Eumaeus, his eyes swollen with emotion, obeyed, and Antinous who was the first to receive the bow exclaimed, 'Stupid swineherd, what are you crying about? Penelope has finally come to a decision and so this wretched business will end. Let me see that bow . . . Hum,' he muttered, 'it will not be easy to draw it . . . It is Odysseus', I remember seeing him with it before he left for Troy. As for me, I am ready and I accept.'

Another Suitor said, 'It seems rather strange though, that a woman should adopt such a test in order to choose her husband.'

'Yes, you are right,' answered another.

Telemachus then rose. 'Men who wish to marry my mother,' he said, his face pale, 'a challenge is put to you. You must accept it and not find excuses to avoid it. Until now you have said that Penelope would not make up her mind. Well, now she has. So it is up to you.' He took off his purple cloak and ordered the maids to bring the axes to him. And all the Suitors rose and watched him, wondering at his precision in lining up the axes in a perfect row.

Followed by her maids, Penelope brought a great bow and a quiver full of arrows.

BOOK XXI

When he had lined up the axes, Telemachus took the bow from Eumaeus and tried to string it . . . but in vain. He tried once more but could not. For the third time he tried to bend the bow . . . and bewildered, he turned to Odysseus, who unseen made a negative sign, meaning, 'No, it is useless, nobody can bend that bow.' With a bitter smile Telemachus said, 'Alas! I am too young or too weak. I cannot do it. But you Suitors who are stronger and more clever than I, here, you try it. No doubt you will succeed!'

He put the bow and arrow down and took his seat. Antinous then rose. 'Come forward my friends! Let us start from the right, that is, the side from which the wine is poured! Let us see which one of us is worthy of the beautiful Penelope!'

The contest began. Leodes was the first. He tried to string the bow . . . two, three times, then gave up saying, 'I am unable to do it, my friends. I admit defeat. May Penelope marry whomever she wishes.' There was a stunned silence in the assembly, but Antinous, impetuously leaping to his feet, exclaimed, 'This bow is too rigid! It must be heated! Come, make a fire!'

Thereupon a fire was lit, the bow was greased with oil in order to make it more supple, and while the Suitors went about their task, silent and intent, Odysseus signalled to Eumaeus and Philoetius, another young swineherd, to follow him. No sooner had they left the hall than he turned to both men and said, 'Eumaeus, Philoetius, tell me frankly. If Odysseus came back now and asked you to fight for him what would be your answer?'

'If Zeus' will could bring back my king, my arms would give you the answer!' replied Eumaeus at once. Then Odysseus, stretching up to his full height and throwing back the hood that covered his face, said, 'Then here I am, it is I, Odysseus! And let me tell you Eumaeus, and you Philoetius that if you help me, I shall regard you both as Telemachus' brothers. Look!' and he showed them the scar on his leg.

The two men were as though they had been struck by lightning, and they fell to their knees in tears. But Odysseus pulled them to their feet and said, 'There is no time for tears or talk now. Eumaeus, go back inside and when the Suitors have finished the contest, you will bring me the bow. First have the maids lock all the doors. You Philoetius, lock the palace gate so that no one can get in or out! Do you understand? . . . Let us go then.' They went back into the palace hall where, in the meantime, Eurymachus had taken hold of the heated and greased bow. He weighed it with a frown, grabbed it in his hand and tried to string it . . . to no avail. A second time, a third time, still in vain.

'Shame on me!' he said, his face flushing. 'Yes shame on me! Not because I can no longer hope to marry Penelope but because I cannot string Odysseus' bow!'

'Come, come!' replied Antinous at once. 'What are you saying? It only means that we have drunk too much today. That's what it means. Or perhaps it is because today is the day of Apollo, the Archer god. Who can imitate him on such a day? No one! Listen to me,' he went on, and the Suitors listened while Penelope smiled a disdainful and mocking smile. 'Let us leave it for today. We will try again tomorrow. We will leave the axes firmly planted in the ground and tomorrow we will try again. You'll see everything will seem easier then. Now let us drink!'

Odysseus took hold of the bow, strung it and drew it back without effort.

'Antinous is right!' they agreed, while the servants filled the cups with wine. Though perturbed, the Suitors started to drink again. After the first cup their discouragement vanished. All right, tomorrow someone would be able to string the wretched bow!

But Odysseus, his hood drawn over his head, then rose and spoke, 'Antinous spoke well and it seems fair to me that the test should be adjourned till tomorrow. But if you will, noble Suitors, allow me to draw the bow myself! I shall not be trying it because I hope to marry the beautiful and wise Penelope . . . but merely to see whether there is still strength left in my arms.' There was a general whisper of scorn 'What?' the Suitors were thinking, 'must we contend with a ragamuffin? . . .'

'Listen old man!' exclaimed Antinous rising to his feet, 'have you gone mad? Is it not enough for you to scrounge off us? What has got into you? Your arms are as weak as any old folks'. Be quiet, eat and don't try to compete

with younger men!'

'Antinous,' interrupted Penelope, 'you cannot treat my guests in this manner. I see no harm in the stranger's request to try and string the bow. What are you afraid of? That I should marry him if he succeeds?' Eurymachus then got up and said, 'No, Penelope it is not that. But if the old ragbag did succeed we would all be humiliated. People would then say, "The Suitors could not string a bow but an old man managed it without effort!" '

'But still,' retorted Penelope, 'if the old stranger wishes to try, I grant him permission to do so!'

While the whispers of discontent from the Suitors continued, Telemachus rose and said, 'Mother, these are men's affairs. I beg you to return to your rooms and leave us to worry about bows and arrows.' Stunned by her son's words, Penelope dared not answer back, so covering her head with her mantle she went back to her rooms followed by her maids. After

a lengthy outburst of grief, she went to sleep, for Athene had poured sweet sleep over her eyes.

In the hall, meanwhile, amongst the protests of the Suitors, Eumaeus, following Telemachus' order, took the bow over to Odysseus who examined it attentively, oblivious to the insults and cries of protest. Nobody had noticed that at a signal from Eumaeus, old Eurycleia had locked the doors!

Shouts and insults subsided. And all, in silence, watched the old man inspecting the bow. Someone said, 'The old man must be an expert!' Suddenly Odysseus grabbed the bow and without effort strung it, making the string vibrate in his fingers. The Suitors held their breath while he calmly notched an arrow. He then drew the string back . . . aimed, released the string and the arrow shot off . . . and did not miss. With a light whistling sound it darted through all twelve rings, and sank into the wall beyond!

BOOK XXII

It all happened within a few seconds. As the stunned Suitors were still staring at the arrow, Odysseus discarded the rags that covered him and, already at his side, Telemachus grabbed a spear and buckled on his sword. Bow in hand Odysseus shouted, 'The contest is over! And now I shall aim at another target!' He lifted the bow, drew the string and let fly an arrow which, with a sinister hiss, pierced Antinous through the throat. The young nobleman collapsed, knocking over his chair. A howl of horror rose from the Suitors and they leapt to their feet. Bumping into each other they rushed to the wall where until a short while ago the weapons had hung . . . They found none. Someone shouted, 'Stranger, have you gone mad? . . .' They still refused to believe that Odysseus had meant to kill Antinous. But notching another arrow, Odysseus thundered, 'You Curs! You thought I would never return home didn't you? Well here I am! Your end has come!'

'Odysseus!' said Eurymachus suddenly, 'listen. You have killed Antinous and he was the instigator. Now that he is dead, justice has been done. I admit we have done wrong. And we shall repay everything we have taken from you. Just allow us to leave!'

Odysseus raised the bow and shot an arrow through Antinous' throat.

'No, nothing can compensate for the offence you have done to me. You have only one choice, to fight or to die! But not one of you shall live!'

Terror struck the Suitors, but Eurymachus, drawing his dagger, shouted, 'Then, my friends, we shall not die without putting up a fight!' and he lunged at Odysseus. Before he could take more than one step an arrow killed him . . . Other Suitors desperately rushed forward, but Telemachus knocked them down with his spear. He then shouted, 'Father, defend yourself, I am going to fetch the weapons!' and while Odysseus shot one arrow after another, Telemachus went out of the hall and came back almost at once with swords and spears. He threw one to Odysseus, the others to Eumaeus and Philoetius, and together they advanced towards the Suitors. These defended themselves as well as they could, with knives and stools, making some sort of barricade with the tables which they had knocked over.

Unexpectedly, Melanthius, a disloyal swineherd who had betrayed his king for these arrogant noblemen, came to their rescue. Melanthius knew the palace well. He went out of the hall, ran to the armoury, took several spears and rushed with them to the Suitors. Now armed, they charged against Odysseus, Telemachus, Eumaeus and Philoetius. Four against so many made an uneven struggle. But Athene appeared by Odysseus' side. 'Where is your strength? Where is the spirit that so repelled the Trojans?' she said to him. Odysseus then let out a cry and flung himself at the Suitors. They attempted to defend themselves . . . but in vain!

Phemius the bard was spared by Odysseus.

'Throw your spears all at the same time!' ordered Odysseus. And Telemachus, Eumaeus and Philoetius launched their spears and knocked down the enemy. The Suitors drew back in disarray to the other end of the hall, but driven by despair they attacked once more. The invisible Athene made all their blows useless. And one by one they all fell in their own blood.

The slaughter was brief. Many Suitors, instead of fighting, had sought escape, but they discovered that the doors were securely barred. Some begged for mercy but Odysseus would not listen to them.

The hall which had held so many merry banquets now resounded with screams, moans and entreaties. Some tried to find shelter under tables, but in vain, for they were driven out and struck down. Together with their lords, the cup-bearers, the bards and the servants were all killed. Odysseus, Telemachus and their faithful swineherds stood erect and bespattered with blood in the centre of the tragic hall where lay so many dead men.

Suddenly a weak voice was heard. '. . . Mercy upon me Odysseus! Spare my life! You shall suffer eternal remorse if you kill me, a mere minstrel, because the gods have taught me to sing and I sing to all men!' It was Phemius the bard.

'It is true,' said Telemachus. 'Spare him father. He is innocent. And if Medon the herald is still alive, spare him too.' At these words the frightened Medon crept out from under an ox hide and implored, 'Telemachus, my boy, protect me!'

'Calm yourself,' said Odysseus. 'You are safe. But now take Phemius with you and go!' Both went out through the door which Philoetius had opened.

Odysseus, followed by Telemachus, walked slowly across the hall to check whether any of the Suitors had escaped his vengeance. No, they were all dead now. 'Telemachus,' he ordered, 'call Eurycleia for me. I must talk to her.' The young man obeyed and soon the old woman appeared on the doorstep of the bloody hall. When she saw the Suitors piled over each other, she let out a fierce cry of joy. But Odysseus exclaimed harshly, 'Restrain yourself, nurse! It is an impious thing to exult over men who have met their death.'

'Yes, yes, Odysseus.'

'Now tell the maids to remove the corpses and clean the hall. Then bring sulphur and fire, for the room must be purified!'

'Yes, my child, I shall bring you a tunic and a cloak,' said Eurycleia, 'for it is unworthy for you to wear these rags!'

'First I want the fire!' ordered Odysseus. And the maids and the servants who had remained loyal rushed in to see their king. They crowded around him clasping his knees.

Eurycleia ran up the stairs of the palace.

BOOK XXIII

Meanwhile Eurycleia hurried up the stairs of the palace. 'Penelope! Penelope!' she cried, going into the room where the queen was still asleep through Athene's spell. 'Penelope come and see! What you have wished for years and years has finally happened. Your husband has come home and has wrought revenge on the Suitors!'

Penelope awoke troubled. 'Are you making fun of me, old woman? Why have you woken me up? Don't you know that sleep is precious to me for it soothes my grief?'

'No, no,' replied Eurycleia wringing her old hands. 'I meant no disrespect. But it is true! Come and see for yourself. Odysseus, the divine Odysseus is back! He is that old man, that stranger with whom you spoke yesterday! Telemachus knew it but kept quiet as he had been ordered!'

The bewildered Queen leapt from her bed. 'Odysseus has returned then?' she exclaimed. 'But how could he fight alone against all the Suitors? . . .'

'I don't know, but I saw that he killed them all.'

'How is that possible, one man alone?'

'Believe me my Queen, I am not lying. Come and see. Come down and you will see that Odysseus is back. Our sorrows are over!'

Immediately, but with shaking hands, Penelope dressed, putting on a cloak. She feared that Eurycleia had taken leave of her senses. She feared another disillusionment. Slowly she walked through the long corridor, all the time trying to stifle the mad flutter of her heart. Thoughts tumbled through her mind. What should she do? Throw herself into Odysseus' arms? . . . But what if that man was not Odysseus, but a god in disguise come to deceive her? Or one more stranger who had got rid of the other Suitors in order to take her away? . . . And how would she be able to recognize her husband in the failing daylight?

Eurycleia told Penelope everything that had happened.

In fact the terrible day was coming to its end and the sun had set. In the palace where the smell of fire and sulphur still lingered, blazing torches had been lit. Now Penelope reached the threshold of the hall and stood quite still. Odysseus was standing with his back to a tall column. She drew closer, then sat before him.

Silence. No-one dared speak. Odysseus waited for Penelope to speak first, but she was not yet convinced that this man covered in rags, still spattered in blood, was the husband for whom she had so longed. Then Telemachus said, 'Mother, is your heart so hard that you do not run to my father? Why do you not speak?'

'My heart is not hard, my son,' Penelope whispered. 'It is only filled with anxiety. And my eyes cannot see well and my voice is too weak to ask questions. But,' she added, 'if this man is really Odysseus returned to his country, then we shall be able to understand each other very well for we share many secrets.'

Hearing this Odysseus smiled and said, 'Your mother speaks true, Telemachus. Go, and leave us alone. Rather, turn your attention to what is happening in Ithaca. The news of the

Penelope ran into Odysseus' arms.

Suitors' death will have spread through the city. Go Telemachus,' he repeated, 'and leave me with your mother. But first,' he added holding him by the arm, 'I want you and everyone in the palace to prepare for a feast. And let the minstrels sing. Do as I tell you!' Telemachus bowed his head and went out. Soon the palace echoed with songs and, as Odysseus had ordered, the faithful servants and cup-bearers started to dance.

Penelope, meanwhile, still did not move. Then Odysseus left the hall in silence and returned soon after, having washed himself of the blood, the dust and the perspiration. He had bathed and put on his best cloak and tunic. He saw that Penelope had not moved and he said, 'Ah! You are indeed hard-hearted Penelope! No other woman would have remained there motionless like you if her husband had come home after an absence of twenty years! Eurycleia,' he added turning to the nurse, 'prepare my bed. I shall sleep alone tonight, seeing that my wife has a heart of stone in her breast.'

'No!' exclaimed Penelope, without rising however. 'I do not have a heart of stone. I know perfectly what you looked like, my husband, when you went to war. Yes, Eurycleia,' she went on, 'prepare Odysseus' bed. Cover it with the most beautiful blankets and take the bed out of his room!'

'Take my bed out of my room?' Odysseus said. 'Impossible! Who could ever move my bed? . . . Nobody, for my bed is but the stump of a huge old olive-tree which still has its roots deep in the earth. Around the bed I built my room. Tell me, Penelope, who can shift such a couch?'

Upon hearing these words Penelope leapt to her feet. 'Odysseus,' she said in a trembling voice, 'my husband, do not be cross with me! I wanted to put you to the test, for if you had been deceiving me I would not have been able to bear it and my heart would have been shattered. Yes, now I know that you are really my husband whom I have loved and for whom I have waited for so long!' And weeping with joy she ran into Odysseus' arms.

Throughout the night Odysseus spoke at length to his wife. He told her everything that had happened to him during the twenty years of his absence. He told her how he had had to face the Cicones and visit the land of the Lotus-Eaters. He told her of his meeting with Polyphemus the merciless Cyclops who devoured some of his most worthy men, and of the hospitality of Aeolius who gave him the leather pouch filled with the winds of the storms . . . Penelope listened, fascinated.

He told her of Circe, the witch goddess who had changed all his companions into pigs. He told her how he was able to enter the kingdom of the dead to consult the soul of Tiresias, and how down there he had met the souls of so many friends who had fallen under the walls of proud Troy, and the ghost of his old mother who had died of grief.

He told her of the Sirens and their songs which enchanted men and lured them to their death; and of the perilous passage between Scylla and Charybdis; and finally how his men, the wretched souls, had slaughtered the sacred cows of Hyperion, bringing down upon them the wrath of the gods.

'. . . and so I remained alone clinging on to a piece of wood in the tempestuous seas. I don't know how I escaped death. I was able to reach the island of the nymph Calypso. She wanted to keep me there for ever; she would have made me immortal, she said, and eternally young. But from the day I left to go to war, I kept in my heart one land and one woman. The land was my country and the woman was you, Penelope.'

So passed the hours of the night and Odysseus was still talking when the stars disappeared one by one and the sky started to turn pink. When the sun rose, Odysseus stood up and said, 'Penelope, I cannot say I have really returned to my land before I hold my old father in my arms. Therefore I shall go to him. I know from Eumaeus that he lives in a hut and tends a small field and an orchard, working like a peasant. I shall go to him, but you must stay here in the palace. Many of the Suitors were nobles of Ithaca, and it is possible that their families are planning revenge. It is best to be on one's guard. Stay in your rooms and do not speak to anyone.'

Penelope promptly obeyed, and Odysseus met Telemachus, Eumaeus and Philoetius. 'Dress for battle!' he ordered. They did as they were told and the four of them, sword on hip and spear in hand, went out of the palace.

Odysseus' father Laertes tended a small field and an orchard.

BOOK XXIV

Walking through the still deserted fields and olive groves on the hills, the group reached the small farm where Laertes had retired after his son had left for the war. Laertes lived in a modest hut with an old maid-servant — the faithful Sicula — and one slave. To them Odysseus said, 'Prepare a banquet and kill the fattest pig you have. Meanwhile I am going to see my father. I want to know whether he recognizes me or not after I have been away for so many years!'

Putting down his weapons, therefore, Odysseus set off for the field where he saw a man on his own, working with his hoe. His heart leapt in his breast, and his eyes filled with tears . . . His father! He was tempted to run to him and embrace him, but he restrained himself and, hiding behind a tree, tried to stifle his emotion. Before revealing himself he thought he would test his father's affection and memory of him. Emerging from behind the tree, Odysseus approached his father.

'Hey, old man,' he said to him 'you seem rather an expert at tending your orchard. I see that the trees are very well cared for and that the flower-beds have been freshly hoed. However,' he added, 'you are the opposite of your orchard.'

'What do you mean, stranger?' replied the startled Laertes.

'What I mean is, you don't look after yourself very well! You are dirty and your wretched clothes add to the ugliness of old age. And yet looking at you more carefully you do not look like a slave. Tell me, is it your master who treats you so badly? And who is indeed your master? Ah, tell me something else. This land on which I have landed, is it really Ithaca? You see,' he went on, 'I used to know a prince who lived on Ithaca, Odysseus was his name. I have never heard anything more of him. I don't know whether he is dead or alive . . . I remember though that he had a father, a good father whose name was Laertes, if I remember rightly. Can you give me any news, old man?'

At these words the old Laertes could not repress his tears. 'Stranger,' he answered, 'you spoke correctly. You have indeed come to the island called Ithaca. Once on this island reigned a valiant and wise man. Now, as you can see it is in the hands of madmen.'

'Madmen? How unfortunate!'

'Unfortunate and sad, yes. But you said you knew Odysseus . . . Tell me, when did you meet him?'

'Why do you want to know?'

'Because I am his father!' Laertes replied. 'Yes, Odysseus was my son. But he is dead now, I am sure, though sometimes I cannot believe it. My son must have died during his homeward journey from Troy, killed on land in some ambush or drowned at sea . . . What a sad fate, without even the comfort of a decent burial!'

'It is impossible to tell what a man's fate was, old man!' replied Odysseus.

'It is true but now we do not hope any more.

whelmed by sorrow and anguish he dropped the hoe and bowed his white head sobbing desperately. Odysseus could not hold back any longer.

'No, my father!' he cried, 'do not weep! I am Odysseus! I am your son!' And Laertes raised his head in alarm and Odysseus clasped him in his arms.

'Do not weep! I am back! And with Athene's help and the assistance of the faithful Eumaeus, the good Philoetius and mostly of Telemachus, I have wrought revenge on the Suitors who offended my wife!'

'Revenge on the Suitors?'

'Yes. None of them are alive father!'

'How is it possible that you did that? . . . Are you not a god under human appearance? . . . or a cruel man who has come to deceive me?'

'I am your son!'

Stepping back, however, the old man asked, 'Are you really my son? . . . One proof,' he added, 'give me one proof so that I may believe you!'

As he had done with Eurycleia, Odysseus uncovered his leg. 'Look father, this wound was made by a wild boar's white tusks when I went hunting on Parnassus. You still do not believe me? Then I will tell you that I remember well the day when you brought me to the orchard when I was still a boy, and in jest you gave me many trees . . . thirteen pear trees, ten apple trees and forty fig trees. You said to me, "I will give you fifty rows of vines which will ripen at different times so that you will have grapes all year round!" '

Then Laertes almost fainted in his son's arms and stuttering he said, 'Yes, yes the gods do exist in Olympus! At last you have come back and you have sought revenge on those who have offended you for so many years! My son, my only hope! But Odysseus, don't you fear the revenge of the Suitors' families?'

'We shall think about that later. Come, my father let us go to your hut. Telemachus and the others are waiting for us.'

So holding each other they went to the hut where their companions were waiting. While Odysseus had a meal with his father there was a

Even Penelope, Odysseus' wife has given up hope. She has remained faithful to him for many years, deceiving her hateful Suitors, her admirers . . . but she will have to decide sooner or later to marry one of them. And then all will be lost for ever,' he concluded mournfully.

Laertes resumed his hoeing, and a while later he asked again, 'But tell me stranger, who are you? Which land do you come from? Have you come on your own ship or did someone bring you here?'

'My name is Eperitus and I come from Alybas,' said Odysseus. But by then he knew that he could not go on like this much longer. He had found out what he wanted to know, that his father too had kept him in his heart and mind.

'And when did you last see Odysseus?'

'Five years ago.'

'Five years!' exclaimed Laertes, and over-

Odysseus, Penelope and Telemachus were at last reunited and happy.

great uproar — screams, laments and questions — in the city. Rumours had spread that the corpses of the Suitors were lying in the palace's courtyard. Their families and friends were gathered at the palace gate and from behind the barred door were asking to be let in, if only to remove their dead.

And so it was done. Among tears and wailing, each family looked for the lifeless body of their kin and took it away. But soon grief and sorrow gave way to anger. 'No, we cannot accept this massacre! If we do not avenge so many young dead, we shall be covered with shame all over Greece!' shouted Eupeithes, Antinous' father.

'What do you want to do then?'

'Let us arm ourselves, look for Odysseus and kill him!'

'Yes, yes!' some shouted, 'put him to death!'

But others, more cautious said, 'No, Odysseus was not wrong to seek revenge. For too long his wife had been insulted and his possessions had been plundered.'

'Without the help of a god,' then exclaimed Phemius, who together with Medon had gone out of the palace, 'Odysseus could not have held out alone against so many enemies!'

'It is true,' confirmed Medon. 'I saw a light by his side! It was Athene! You cannot fight against Athene!'

'Athene will not stop us!' shouted Eupeithes, and with a group of armed men he set off towards Laertes' hut, for he knew that Odysseus had gone there. Civil war was about to break out on Ithaca. Was then Odysseus' return to trigger off an endless succession of vengeances? . . .

No. Athene had heard everything and seen everything. And turning to Zeus she asked what was to be the will of the father of all gods and men. Zeus answered, 'May Odysseus reign in peace. May the dead be forgotten and peace, wisdom and prosperity return to Ithaca, as before!' Athene returned to the island just at the moment when Odysseus, having armed himself in haste, was running his terrible spear through Eupeithes. But this was to be the last death because a blinding thunderbolt was sent down from heaven by Zeus as a warning, and Athene calmed the lust for revenge.

And so weapons were set aside and hands were shaken in reconciliation. And Odysseus' return marked the start of a new era of peace and happiness in Ithaca.

152